THE MODERN YOU – UNCOVER P3

Principles, Patterns, and Practices to achieve your Dreams.

First published: March 2019

ISBN-13: 978-0-578-48168-5

Please send us your feedback, comments, and suggestions! by email to

UncoverP3@dreambigbuddy.com

www.dreambigbuddy.com

Dedication

To my parents, Mr. V Asokaraju & Mrs. A Thulasi.

To my better half Bhuvanya and my two daughters, Yasha and Kavina.

To my coach & CEO Mr. Sam Ramasamy.

To my closely traveling friend Suresh Kumar.

To all my virtual role models.

Contents

Foreword

As an organizational designer, I frequently have had the opportunity to observe individuals who learn, grow, lead and succeed in their respective careers. While most leaders stop here, Naren has taken the next action that is seldom taken – the step of giving back! He has found a way to give back and pass on his learning to the next generation with this masterpiece called The Modern YOU – Uncover P3.

This book by Naren is a labor of love. The Modern You was an outcome of his reflective notes to self. Why is Naren's thoughtful notes to himself so engaging to anyone who reads his notes? It is because he is one of us. He is one of the few among us who took accountability for his actions and pushed hard through multiple challenges to accomplish his dreams including writing this book.

Seldom have I been inspired and moved by a book as I have with the one that you are holding in your hand right now. The clarity of thought, the simplicity of application and brevity in communication will propel you to action.

In the words of former South African President Nelson Mandela, "Education is the most powerful weapon which you can use to change the world." This book in addition to educating you, will move you to action. It is part self-help, part reflection and more importantly has little nuggets in every chapter that you will be intrinsically inspired. What you get out of this book will not be something that Naren would dictate. What you get out of this book will be a reflection of your own self!

The book will help you hold a mirror to your face. Help you see what you knew about yourself but seldom dared to acknowledge. Everyone gets a fair chance in life. If you wondered about how to be prepared to make the most of the opportunities presented to you in life, this book would give you a framework to do just that - to be better prepared and ready to seize the day. Each of the four sections in the book will provide you with the opportunity to gain clarity on finding new paths to redesign your life for success. Are you ready to embark on this adventure to achieve your dreams?

This message in this book is something you will want to share with your friends who have big aspirations like you. Enjoy the nuggets just like you would savor your favorite warm brownies. It is that good.

Then, pass it on.

Bala V Sathyanarayanan

Fellow Traveler

Westport, CT

Preface

Does anybody not want to make the most out of their life?

We all want more vacation, more fun, more money, more time, better lifestyle, and more, but, at the same time, we want to work less.

We are in the age where there is an abundance of information but a deficit of attention. Can our expectation to have more in life be traded for anything? No way...

Every human has basic needs and prime needs.

One has to struggle when one's basic needs like food, clothes, and shelter are not met. When one's prime needs like growth, connection, and autonomy are not satisfied, one feels unhappy, demotivated, and depressed.

So, the big question is: Is there a key to achieving these basic and prime needs with ease?

Humans have come through a long journey from survival to living in comfort and luxury. Our evolution has lots of pointers, which one can use to speed up the process of achieving one's dreams.

It's time to answer the hardest question:
Where or what are those pointers to achieving the dream life each of us deserves?

*"To make an impact and achieve your dream life, you must first understand **"The Modern YOU"** in full".*

When I first started learning the core principles, I realized that those principles revealed certain pathways and techniques. Intrigued by the possible results of those pathways, I started practicing the techniques, and in a very short time, they helped me reveal the map I wanted to travel. I grouped those techniques and presented them as patterns in this book.

Once I embarked on my journey, I was able to start enjoying the fruits of work more often as it boosted my confidence to a much higher level to do more and have fun.

First of all, this is the book I wanted for myself to clarify my thoughts for the journey of achievements I wanted to have. Feeling that it is going to be very helpful for all, I wanted to publish the same to the world, utilizing the power of the Internet: the infinite network, which is available to virtually all people. Therefore, this is me, achieving my first goal of writing a book, which can assist all in achieving their goals. Hooray!!!

Aspirant Noticeboard:

What is in this book: Principles to understand the different aspects of life and tactical patterns to synthesize and achieve your dream.

How long it will take to read: a maximum of 10 minutes per chapter.

Real-time applicability: Packed with pointers to apply it on a day-to-day basis for one's journey to achieve big.

How much benefit will be reaped – from seed to a huge tree. Your time is the seed.

Knowing that every young aspirant going to high school or college nowadays is tasked with a lot more complicated projects, I am positive that the material in this book is a helpful guide at this juncture than ever before for every high schooler, college student, millennial, or anybody who has the ambition to achieve something.

Give it a try:

It will take about 3 to 4 hours max to read the whole book cover to cover, which is about the same time it takes to watch 2 full movies.

Do you want to trade the time it takes to watch 2 movies for life-changing practical wisdom to achieve your dream life?

You have 2 choices:

Choice 1: Watch 2 movies and continue on your current path.

Choice 2: Go out of the box – give a try to this book, see a different perspective, uncover new paths, and design your life for success.

As always, the choice is yours.

For the time worth spent, my recommendation is Choice 2.

Please, provide me a chance to show you *"The Modern YOU"* in the format of:

The Modern You – Uncover P3 – Principles, Patterns, & Practices

As an author, I request you to pay attention to every chapter and practice the patterns for a minimum of 1 to 3 months to see the positive changes it will bring in you, through which you will experience more determination in achieving the goal you set forth for yourself.

This book is not a religious or spiritual reference. Instead, it is packed with practical wisdom for the current era and the stories I have are true, and are from my own experiences, which I have used to enhance the subject I want to emphasize.

Target Audience & Book Organization

This was written primarily for those who are ready to talk consciously about what they want to do when they grow up and are working towards achieving their goals.

In my opinion, 9th graders and older would be the most able to digest these concepts and start applying them towards their success.

I highly recommend this book for high schoolers, college students, fresh graduates, and millennials looking for direction, or just anybody who wants a prescription of steps which can serve as a harness for them not to deviate from their goals and help to focus on achieving their goals.

This book will help you in defining your destiny and also will provide you with a map of how to achieve it.

Book Organization

This book is organized into four sections.

Section 1: Principles which will provide a deeper understanding of important concepts such as Life, Skill, Time, Money, Adaptability, New Normals, Moral Loan, and lots more.

Section 2: Patterns which I created, followed, and tweaked over the last few years, which helped me in achieving my goals quickly and provided the guidance and confidence for the long journey ahead. Measuring growth is the core value proposition of all these tools which will lead to long-term success. The patterns are organized into four categories: Prime Growth, Watchdog, Driver and Motivational. Also included is a full chapter dedicated to explaining the yogic practices in a simplified form, which any person can adapt to their advantage.

I can 100% assure you that the time you invest in learning and implementing these patterns and practices will be worth it.

Section 3: This section contains a practical and detailed run through of the application of the patterns and the practices in the making of this book.

Section 4: Closing – Question to Self, and The Power of Dream.

Appendix: Headstream – Dreambigbuddy coding club

__Infographics -__ 1-page graphical illustration to understand the scope of the book.

The Modern You - Uncover P3

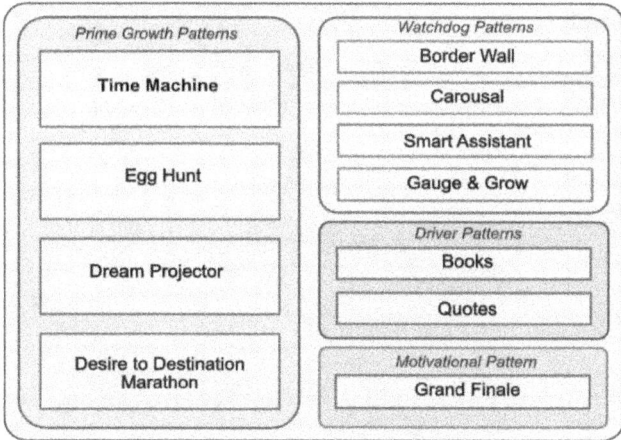

Prime Growth Patterns	Watchdog Patterns
Time Machine	Border Wall
	Carousal
	Smart Assistant
Egg Hunt	Gauge & Grow

	Driver Patterns
Dream Projector	Books
	Quotes

	Motivational Pattern
Desire to Destination Marathon	Grand Finale

Yogic Practices for common Man
Strengthen Mind, Body & Soul

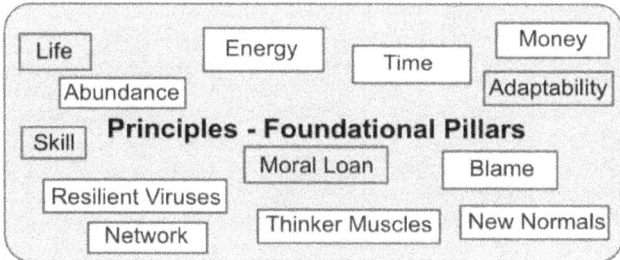

Life   Energy   Time   Money

Abundance   Adaptability

Skill   **Principles - Foundational Pillars**

Moral Loan   Blame

Resilient Viruses   Thinker Muscles   New Normals

Network

SECTION 1 - PRINCIPLES

Introduction – Principles

Every person or organization who has achieved something had three important things defined for them to direct their journeys:

Vision, Mission, and Values.

Vision: What you want to be seen as when you achieve your life goal.

Mission: What the immediate goal is that will be achieved – the stepping stone for the grander vision.

Values: What will guide you to make the right decisions in your journey towards achieving the goal.

We all wish to achieve big things. If those three are the fundamentals, do you have them precisely defined for yourself?

The principles explained in this section are discrete concepts which will help you in <u>providing direction,</u> as well as help in defining the vision, mission, and values for your journey of success.

Life is a Gift

When **God Murugan** wanted to test **Avvaiyar,** one of the greatest poets who lived during the 2nd century CE, he asked:

What is Rare?

Great Avvaiyar responded to that question through a poem in the Tamil language:

"அரியது கேட்கின் வரிவடி வேலோய்!

அரிதரிது மானிடர் ஆதல் அரிது

மானிடராயினும் கூன் குருடு செவிடு பேடு நீக்கிப் பிறத்தல் அரிது"

In the above verse, she explained

Being born as a human is rare. In spite of that rare creation, being born with features such as a straight spine, not blind, not deaf and not mute, is rarer than being just born.

We must visualize the things science explains to us. Billions of years ago, there was a BIG BANG!! From there, galaxies formed and within themselves, stars and planets were created. The Planet Earth is so unique, in its size, distance from the sun, and overall composition, which allows it to support life, which took several millions of years to form.

On top of all these phenomenons, various generations of evolution, from single-cell to multi-cell to animal forms, led to the rise of the human species.

Hypothetical question: – if the huge asteroid which struck the earth and killed the dinosaurs didn't happen at all, what would have happened to the human race? Would the dinosaurs have eaten us all?

Humans are the only species with all the rare features, especially the ultimate ***sixth sense***, which enables them to think and achieve the dream life that they want.

With the power of the sixth sense in the last 100 years, we humans have come up with several innovations to overcome most of the disabilities our race faces today. With these empowerments, we are living in a time where everything is possible. We are able to prove to ourselves that humans are extremely special, beyond our imagination.

Close to nine million species living in this world and we, the humans, are the only species gifted to have this miraculous power, the sixth sense. In the world, the total human population is nearing eight billion people, do you realize each one is unique? Each human being is a unique creation among trillions of living organisms in this world.

Our existence in this world is very rare. We should feel blessed for our mere existence.

Which brings us to a very important question, why are we given this opportunity to live with such a great gift?

What is expected out of each of us?

There are only two ways to live your life. One is as though nothing is a miracle.The other is as though ***everything*** is a ***miracle***.
-Albert Einstein

Skill

How many times, knowingly or unknowingly, have we told ourselves that "I CAN'T do it"?

From childhood, there have been many things we are able to do after some kind of practice, such as cycling, swimming, playing a new game, cooking, dancing, etc.

There are many research studies that show it takes 10,000 hours of training to master a specific skill. If you really ask the question of what these studies were trying to prove, they were studying the people who really achieved mastery in a particular skill and reached very high levels using that skill. Some examples are Michael Jackson, A.R. Rahman, Magic Johnson, etc.

Similar kinds of studies were undertaken to find out the **minimum hours of** practice one needs to **learn a NEW SKILL** and feel proud.

You will be very surprised to know the answer, which is a mere **20 hours** of commitment. That is just a 1-hour commitment each day, which equates to a new skill every month, even if we exclude weekends!

WOW – any **SKILL** can be learned within 20 hours of committed training and a focus to achieve it.

What if you were told that *everything is a skill,* not an inborn quality or a gift? This opens us to a whole universe of opportunities for those who are willing to

Skill

give it a try and commit just 20 hours of effort to learn a new skill.

Competency Ladder: Mastering a skill goes through four phases of competence as depicted in the following diagram. This theory of "Four Stages for Learning any New Skill" was developed by Noel Burch in 1970.

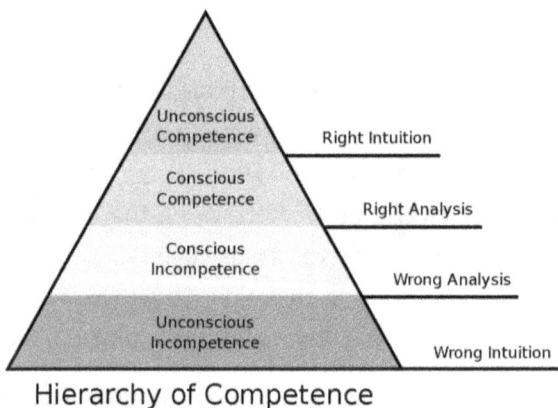

Hierarchy of Competence

By understanding the four levels, one can easily overcome any kind of mental obstacles in the path of acquiring a new skill.

- The first stage (red) from the bottom is called Unconscious Incompetence. At this level, one doesn't understand the purpose of a skill and doesn't recognize that they even lack that skill and its usefulness.
- The second stage (yellow) is called Conscious Incompetence. At this level, one recognizes

that they lack a skill by understanding its usefulness.

- The third stage (green) is the Conscious Competence. At this level, one makes an effort to acquire the skill and is able to perform in a way that they can be proud of. <u>*One can cross the first 3 stages by investing* **20 hours** *of time*</u> towards acquiring a particular skill.

- The fourth stage (blue) is the Unconscious Competence. At this level, one practices the skill so much that they are able to master the skill, so that it becomes second nature, and it can be performed without even much effort.

I **strongly** believe:

Any skill learned early on, can take you to miraculous destinations, which you never dreamed of.

When was the last time, in the recent past, you explored something new, which you never did before?

In the last 1 week, did you acquire a new skill? If "YES", you are awesome!!!

If "NOT"

How about in the last 1 month?

How about in the last 3 months?

How about in the last 6 months?

How about in the last 1 year?

How about in the last 5 years?

How about in the last 10 years?

When you read the above lines, you might be wondering why I am kind of asking the same type of question for different periods of time.

The more times you answered "NO" shows that you are getting **rusty** and that it is time to brush up and give yourself a chance to be ready for what is needed from you.

Being ready is of utmost importance. You will regret or sometimes be forced if you are not ready,

The 10 skills you need to master to succeed are:

1. Being honest about yourself
2. Being Innovative – Connect the dots
3. Being Adaptable
4. Having confidence –Seeing things positively
5. Listening
6. Public speaking
7. Managing your time
8. Living in the present moment – Not past, Not future
9. Being consistent
10. Having empathy

Rate yourself on each skill on a scale of 1 to 10, starting from 1 as a beginner to 10 as a master. Work towards achieving mastery of each skill to achieve great success in your life.

Spending life miserably is EASY,
Practicing Happiness is a SKILL!!

Energy

Have you noticed there are times when we have high energy and times of low energy?

What is causing these highs and lows?

If you notice which activities:

- *kindle our curiosity,*
- *provide a direct or indirect result,*
- *provide a connection,*
- *provide an edge, or*
- *are just plain fun and enjoyable,*

We are involved and do those activities with high energy. All <u>others</u> are dealt with using low energy.

My uncle Dr. G. Alagar Ramanujam, former professor of physics, college principal, and metaphysics researcher, visits the USA every year and conducts seminars on Vethathirian principles, illuminating all. His recent work is on what happened before the Big Bang, and whether the Big Bang really happened. Additionally, he started an Ashram in Tanjore, India. Furthermore, he consistently publishes a magazine every month. He dedicates a good portion of his life to helping the people in and around that location.

I am lucky enough to have spent a good time with him every year for the last few years. He is in his 80's and is doing all this work and has a huge plan to do more. But, where is he drawing this huge amount of energy from?

Driving a technology team in my organization over many years, I have introduced processes such as Scrum, TDD, new technology projects, and I am currently working on implementing the Domain-driven design. I have always been involved in these endeavors.

When I am writing this book, I am bursting with a high energy rush.There is a similar burst, when I do weekly evening classes for kids on technology through the "Headstream – Dream Big Buddy Coding Club".

But why is the energy very high while doing these activities?

I am sure everybody has their own areas where energy is very high and areas where it is low.

The first law of thermodynamics, also known as the Law of Conservation of energy, states that :

Energy is neither created nor destroyed,
but it can be transformed from one form to another.

This brings us to the biggest revelation to all, that energy is there. We have to learn to tap into it and use it to our advantage.

If you notice there is a common thread flowing in all the above examples, which is nothing but the **Purpose – WHY** we are doing these activities, that kindle the energy system. I am sure there are several things you can correlate similarly to the situations above in your life.

Identify the **Purpose – WHYs in your life** and work on those to succeed.

Asking yourself and considering the WHYs in your life will bring about a new tool: <u>**curiosity**</u>. You can employ curiosity to explore different things and to narrow a purpose for which your efforts are worth investing in. Curiosity will kindle your energy system.

Time

People are much busier than ever before.

With the boom of the internet, everything is very accessible and available at our fingertips instantly. Every media is fighting for our time, and they all want to keep us for as long as they can.

It has been calculated that 80% of our active time is spent on social media, the internet, and TV, while only 20% of our active time is spent on productive work. Checking social media is a serious drain of our time in our current century, which steals our resources without us realizing it. Also, it makes us be in the reactive mode all the time – we are influenced to do things based on the posts/feeds we come across, instead of our plan to do what we wanted.

Distractions are the procrastination monkey of your mind, which makes you delay things even though you know it is a waste. These distractions are stopped by a forceful reality called a **deadline**. Until we get closer to a deadline, this monkey makes us waste our time. Using the pattern, *"Desire to Destination: D2D Marathon"*, we can help fix this problem, which I will be explaining in detail under Section 2: Patterns and Practices.

For instance, let's assume life is fair and everybody is going to live for 100 years. Take a sheet of paper and put 10 small boxes in each row, and repeat 10 times.

In the end, you should have 100 total boxes. Each box represents 1 year of age. Shade the number of boxes as per your age. Maybe you are past 1/5 or 1/4 or 1/3 or half of the total allocated life. If you think about it, it all flew like a day or week – so fast, isn't it? Can you visualize how soon the remaining is going to go? And realistically, we also know life is not fair, and that it varies for every person.

It takes at least 3-5 years, maybe even 10 years, for a business or any big project to be stabilized and to reap its benefits.

On average, everybody goes through a learning stage of 16 to 25 years to even take a shot at doing something.

Assuming you are starting any project in your early twenties, you can have a maximum of 5 chances, even if you fail to achieve 4 times. If you are smart, lucky and provide the right ingredients for your project, you may reach your success early on, but that is not guaranteed. So don't wait to get started.

One fair thing in the world is, everybody has the same amount of time in a day (24 hours/ 1440 minutes) in spite of who they are. With all the things happening around us, each day that we wake up is a gift of its own, which we need to embrace.

Value of Time:

Time = Exponent of your current self into future
Time = Traded Opportunity Cost

How and where you spend your given time is the critical decision you need to constantly make to ensure that the odds of success are in your favor.

The rich can invest money, but the poor can only invest Time.

"Time is free, but it's priceless.
You can't own it, but you can use it.
You can't keep it, but you can spend it.
Once you've lost it you can never get it back."
-Harvey MacKey

This whole book is written utilizing my spare time available in the evenings and at the weekends. I feel very achieved on this usage of time.

When I started using the tool *"Time Machine"* *(which I will be explaining in detail under "Section 2: Patterns and Practices"),* I began to see the drains of time, and realized how I can channel that time effectively to my advantage to achieve my goals, for which I previously never found time to do, because I wrongly thought I was super busy.

Multitasking is not a skill or power, but instead, is a drainer. Prioritize and uni-task to utilize time to the fullest and not waste time on regaining your train of thought.

Multiplying TIME is a SKILL – you can gain that skill by **automating**, **delegating** or **simply answering the**

question: *do you really need to do a particular thing or not?*

Saying "YES" to a thing will automatically imply saying "NO" to many other things. Those things will have to be delayed or cannot be done.

Time can be created only for what you really want, but what you want is a choice. The choice may be personal or forced.

"If you don't make the time to work on creating the life you want, you're eventually going to be forced to spend a LOT of time dealing with a life you don't want."
– Kevin Ngo

Money

Money is made only by <u>creating value</u> for the consumers utilizing your services.

95% of the world population trade their time for money, whether it's a full-time, part-time, or consultant job.

As long as you work for somebody, you are trading your time for money. Bottom line – if you cannot work, you don't get paid. The luxury that you enjoy is, you do not have to worry about managing a business and handle other activities – you simply deliver the work and get paid for the time.

On the other hand, business owners not only get paid for the time they invest, but also get returns on their investments as profits. Even though it sounds nice, it has its own risks. The advantage of owning a business is that it can make money even if the owner themselves is not working, depending on how the business is designed.

If you have never started a business and wanted to explore the internal workings of a business, the only way to do it is to start one. Don't worry whether it is going to fail or succeed.

Now the questions are: What to do? What about the investment? And where do I start?

Money

To learn or experiment a business, my recommendation would be to think of putting up a lemonade stand on a weekend, as it would be a great way to expose anyone to understand the concepts of business, at a very small cost.

Let us assume we are starting with a loan of $20.

Start with the things we need to set up a lemonade stand:

- How to put up the stall
- How to attract customers
- How to serve
- What is the cost of each cup of lemonade?
- How to organize the whole day of sales
- How long will we sell

After one day of sales, ask:

- How much money did we get from sales?
- Did we make money or lose money?
- Can we pay back the loan?
- If we want to continue the lemonade stand for the next day, can we use the learning from day 1?

Disclaimer: Some states have a restriction on setting up lemonade stands and require an earlier approval from local authorities for clearance, so just be aware of the rules and handle as needed.

The wisdom you can acquire through this process will definitely be worth the investment.

I have dedicated a separate chapter to explain this concept: **Entrepreneurship**.

The money you make is not what you think you deserve, it is what the consumer is willing to pay for your services. But on the contrary, if you or your services are in demand, you can set your own prices.

When we come across a situation where we are underpaid for our services, we have a few choices: learn the gaps and provide better services, showcase to the customer the value of your services, or just accept that you might be in the wrong place rendering your services.

A few years ago, I had to borrow some money from a known source. I was returning the money in chunks and it took almost 3 years for me to settle the loan. When I finished the amount, the person who lent the money to me asked for another big chunk towards interest. I didn't expect this and I was in shock, as that was never discussed. Up until that moment, I had also lent money to others and had never taken any interest, since I was giving and taking in a known circle. This is the moment I realized, you cannot assume with money. You have to be explicit.

Ignorance is expensive.

In this experience, I learned what simple and compound interest are. Some lessons cost money. But I was able to negotiate and reduce the interest.

This led to three very important lessons:

> ***Money is not free.***
> ***Money is negotiable.***
> ***Money can work & can grow by itself when rightly invested.***

Paper money depreciates in value over time. An item you got a few years ago versus buying the same item now, has increased in cost over time. If you are holding paper money, you have to spend more money for the same item now.

> ***Money doesn't grow on trees, but***
> ***if you sow the right seeds, you can reap money.***

The way you can grow money is by utilizing proper investment options, such as property, which can yield rent, shares or mutual funds which can yield returns, and/or create products which can produce royalties. Find the right investment options and continue to care for it, so that it can work for you even when you are not doing work and can grow by itself.

All commodities depreciate in value, whether it is a car, a phone, or any item. On the contrary, we enjoy it. Be cognizant of what and where you are spending money.

If you are starting a business, try to work out ways to grow the business organically. Sometimes, raising money looks needed, but it does come with a COST – be aware of the effects.

Investment Gotchas:

- Money put in the bank – in checking and savings accounts – doesn't grow. But it is a good way to limit spending by not keeping it in hand. The interest rates on those accounts may be less than 1% annually.
- Safe growth instruments – bonds, pension funds – have 3% to 5% annual growth as well as possible tax benefits.
- Long-term investments for a medium and high growth – investing in property or gold.
- Investing in shares/ mutual funds may produce high gain or high loss depending on one's understanding of the market conditions.
- Don't blindly bet on luck to make more money, when you are making stock market investments.
- Very high risk – CAUTION – Some investments promise 25% or double or triple more growth in a very short time.
  - Understand the risk of what will happen when you fully lose it.
  - Some of the examples are unorganized investment plans, like Bitcoin trading.
- Insurance – technically not true investment options, but there are 2 types: Term insurance costs less but has no returns and growth Unit-linked insurance plans will cost high but provides some returns.

- o   Understand the clauses clearly and use based on your needs.
- o   Term insurance is a way to create a safety net if you are not going to be around to take care of your dependants.

Money = Choices

Money provides more options to choose from.

Do not waste time arguing whether money is good or bad. Money can provide comfort, security, and freedom, but it may not provide all the happiness. However, <u>by not having money</u>, it is guaranteed that life is going to be tough.

While money can buy happiness, it cannot prevent sadness.

Money is the world accepted form of legal tender to get things for its equivalent monetary value.

The Stone Age is long gone. We are now in the Currency Age.

Money is required for:

- Survival
- A safety net to handle an emergency situation
- Retirement time – the age which we will not have enough energy and strength to do work

- Exploration – Fun, Travel, Experiences, Family
    - Humans by nature, are explorers, and the more we explore, the more we will be motivated to achieve new heights.
    - You have shoes to fit all sizes – enjoy your size before you are in need of the next size

In the world, two-thirds of billionaires are 1st generation, which means that the majority of them are self-made and didn't inherit wealth from their parents.

Poverty is a lifestyle, not fate.

Being poor can definitely be changed if the right action is taken. Money is a resource, but that is not the only resource to become successful.

An **idea** has **zero value** until it makes money.

Talking is cheap if it is not combined with action that shows results.

Abundance

During my middle school years (1988 – 1993), every summer vacation my parents took my brother and I to visit my grandparents' who lived in a nice little town called Tirunelveli in South India. We took the train from our home in Chennai and traveled almost 12 hours to reach Tirunelveli. These train travels were by far, the best part of the trip, as I loved to look outside and see farmlands, landscapes, mountains, the waving people, reading the station names and the merchants selling local market items at every station. By the time I reached my grandparents' house, I would have lots of questions about different train engines, and even how the train pulls so many compartments. With my grandpa being a retired station master, he was always eager to tell stories of how railway stations, trains, and how other related things work.

During one of these trips, I noticed there were 4 lines of metal cables following along the tracks of the railway line. I was curious why they were laid like that and what they did. When I asked about that, my grandpa told me about the telegraph and how it works. I was very surprised at how the information traveled from one point to another and how there were people to transfer that information at every station, each almost 75 kilometers apart because the information could not be transmitted over long distances.

Around 1998-99, when I was in my 3rd year of college, I got a telegraph message saying that my grandma "expired" and I had to go to Tirunelveli to participate in the final ceremony. Although my college is just 200 kilometers away from my grandparents' house, this message was sent in the morning and I got it late in the afternoon. Even though it was delayed, I still got to attend the final ceremony. Dial tone phones were available, but they were not accessible. Cell phones were not even known to the general public at that time.

Twenty years since then, with the introduction of the internet and wireless technology, everybody is now carrying a device in their hands and getting instant messages. We can even see the other person typing. We have a personal assistant, travel guide, and route map to tell which direction to go, all in our hands and available all the time. My kids talk to their grandparents every week through video chat the second we want to see each other. What a great empowerment technology has provided to all of our lives!

Now the whole world is hyper-connected. You can search for anything and find the answers. Consumers are connected to the manufacturers very easily. Global trade is happening at a very high pace and on a large scale. There are so many ways available to publish your thoughts to the world community instantly, by using the Internet through tweets, blogs, and social media platforms like Facebook, WhatsApp, and Snapchat. As things are happening, we can better understand the realities of the other side.

Billions of people, like never before, are connected through a single, great network called the "World Wide Web", commonly known as the "Internet".

Realize the immense power that the Internet can provide us with, and the infinite possibilities we all want.

What a great time in human history that we are gifted to live in!!!

Creativity and the power of the internet led to several businesses flourishing around us in a very short time span of 10 years, such as Google, Facebook, Uber and many more.

With the innovations happening in *cloud computing technologies*, everything is made accessible to all to achieve anything at a very affordable cost and in a short time.

Still, there is a huge vacuum to be filled and it is up to each one of us to take our chance to fill it.

Are you up for the challenge to utilize the abundance and show your ART to this world?

Adaptability

"Survival of the fittest" is the phrase coined by Herbert Spencer when he started visualizing his economic theories, which aligned with Darwin's biological and evolutionary theories.

In 2000, while I was in my final year of college, there was a huge lottery for the college graduates fueled by the internet boom in the advanced countries. Because of that, many multinational IT organizations were hiring fresh grads from colleges at a high rate in India. I was one of those lucky ones to directly get the job through campus interviews and was placed in the job as soon as I graduated from college to work as a software engineer with an attractive salary package.

We were treated like we were gifted in the office and were provided with the latest technologies in the market. As the days went by, we were deployed to internal product developments to sharpen our skills, so that when there is a need, we will be sent to the USA or the UK or any of the other places we all dreamed to get our flight tickets for.

September 11, 2001 – 9/11 – The attack on the Twin Towers in New York by terrorists was an unimaginable event for the entire mankind at the time, and impacted everybody in the world. This was one of the major factors that triggered the internet bubble to burst and suddenly, all the multinationals needed to start chopping their workforce to control their expenses.

During this time, I saw many of my senior colleagues, who had a lot of IT experience and were really good at mainframes, got laid off. Although they were skilled, they didn't learn the latest technologies at that time. They thought companies should take care of them, but that didn't last for long and most of them were asked to leave the company because they were a big expense to the organization mainly because they were <u>unable to adapt</u> to the new technology trends quickly.

When Apple introduced the iPod, which could store 1000's of songs in a very small device, this disruption put a lot of music player giants to the ground because they were not able to adapt to the change.

Nokia was a popular phone company until 2007. When iPhones were introduced, the whole company went out of business because they were not able to introduce a successful, new phone. Blackberry's and Windows' phone tried to adapt for a long time, but unable to compete, many divisions were closed.

Similar things happened and continued to happen in all fields – whoever was not able to adapt to the environment became outdated and vanished.

"Where there is a danger, a rescuing element grows as well" – Friedrich Hölderlin

Microsoft, a great company for years, started to go downhill around 2008. When new CEO Satya Nadella took over, he quoted "Our industry does not respect tradition — it only respects innovation". Within a few years under his leadership, he brought several changes that led the company back to its high glory by adapting to the latest trends in every aspect as well as delivering for today's needs and the future.

"Survival of the fittest":

Theorized more than 150 years ago and it still holds good today.

<u>Adaptability is a very important skill</u> everyone must possess to continue to have a good ride throughout our lifetime. The only way you can adapt is through consistent learning and by evaluating positions regularly.

Thinker Muscles

The most powerful function of the human is the executive decision-making power, the power to think and do what the individual wants, and in most cases, achieve higher than the individual's physical capacity, and not just for mere survival.

These executive functions usually arise from the brain, but at times, from the stomach muscle called the "gut" – a strong feeling we believe it will work even though others feel it will not – and at times from the feelings inside the "heart" to pursue.

These 3 muscles – ***Brain, Gut and Heart*** – are the thinker muscles in our body that help in making us live a superior life.

For any muscle to become stronger, you need to perform routine exercises with it. The same is also applicable to "Thinker Muscles". One should make the thinker muscles stronger and smarter by participating in continuous learning, trying new things, and also keeping the physical body healthy.

Together, the function of these 3 muscles forms the mind.

A strong mind lives in a strong body.

Qualities of the mind:

- Makes judgments quickly
- What you have chosen to get is what you get
- What you visualize as the future becomes your reality
- Likes pleasure, not pain
- Always chooses familiar things as the first option even though there may be better options out there

By understanding the above qualities and tweaking when needed to steer away from the wrong direction, we can make our thinker muscles stronger and more direct to execute smarter.

Belief:

Beliefs are the products of the choices you have made and the events that happened in your life. Your life experiences create your belief system.

Beliefs shape our lives. They are so powerful that they can drive an individual in a positive or negative direction. Questioning the beliefs will provide a realization of one's own self.

What are the beliefs you have about yourself, life, family, friends, work, future, death, after death?

Why do you have those beliefs?

Is what you believe in sync with what you want?

If what you believe is not what you want, what are the changes you need to make to ensure your belief is in sync with what you want?

Being true to your inner self to the above questions can provide clarity to your destiny and asking this more regularly will help you self-correct the path you are traveling to achieve your wants.

Emotions:

The eight basic emotions are: joy, surprise, trust, anticipation, fear, anger, sadness, and disgust.

Understanding that *fear and anxiety are just feelings and not reality* can help in boosting self-control to better handle a situation.

Fear freezes action.

If you want to induce action, you need to create a world for yourself which provides quick gains.

Gains should be a social incentive, have an immediate reward and showcases progress.

Anger is the outcome when the expectations are not met. Normal behavior is to react with retaliation.

Amygdala, the right side of the brain, processes fear, triggers anger, and motivates us to act. It alerts us in times of danger and activates the "fight or flight" response. The right side of the brain tries to judge whether a current situation is hazardous by comparing that situation with your collection of past memories. If it vaguely matches a previous negative event, your brain immediately raises warning sirens.

Researchers have also found that the prefrontal cortex (front part of the brain) controls reasoning, judgment and helps us think logically before we act.

Whether you can have your Amygdala react or prefrontal cortex act in a situation is determined by how much control you have over your brain.

The brain is a complex organ which can be tweaked for an advantage when you understand its functions and be in complete control of the situations you face.

You can practice attaining a steady state of mind by being aware of your surroundings and being able to let things go. Meditation will definitely help to achieve that steady state of mind. I have a simplified practice prescribed under "Section 2- Yogic Practices" to get a greater control of the mind.

Feedback:

We constantly receive comments from different sources about us, about the work we deliver and many other things. Depending on what we receive, from whom we receive and why we receive, we process those feedbacks differently.

When we receive feedback, we either feel positive, agitated or neutral.

How we feel about the feedback is only half of the equation. How we want to use the feedback and how we want to respond to those feedbacks is the other half and that reaction is completely your choice.

The choice of action we take will fall under any one of the following:

- Attack
- Self-doubt
- Expand
- No action

Think about the things that have happened to you and the kind of decisions you arrived at and if it could have been done differently.

A comparison is a form of feedback we do knowingly or unknowingly, and most often it demotivates rather than being an advantage for the individual growth. Understanding the negative talker from within or outside, and ensuring to stay away from those will help to focus on the growth rather than going into the negative spiral of self-depression.

Instant gratification:

The "pleasure principle" is the driving force that compels human beings to gratify their needs, wants, and urges.

> *"What decides the purpose of life is simply the program of the pleasure principle."*
> – Sigmund Freud, Austrian neurologist

Instant gratification is the desire to experience pleasure or fulfillment without delay or deferment. In other words, it's when you want something, and you want it at that time.

When we don't get fulfillment, our psychological response is anxiety or tension.

Because of this nature, we may end up making unexpected expenses and mistakes.

Knowing that instant gratification is just a feeling that can be subsided when questioned, will help us to be in control of the mind.

Ask the following questions and try to answer them when there is a sudden urge to do things. It is not easy, but if you can answer them and the need still exists, go ahead and pursue it. If you decide not to pursue it, you may save yourself from a waste of time, energy, and money.

Do I really need it or is it just a luxury or an impulsion?

Do I need it now or can it wait?

Which options exist?

Once the need is satisfied or subsided, it is not the end. You are still going to get a new gratification sooner or later.

"Instant gratification begets instant gratification."
– Neil Patel in Entrepreneur Network

Instant gratification can be a powerful tool when rightly used.

DiSC is a behavior assessment tool based on the DISC theory of psychologist William Moulton Marston, which centers on four different behavioral traits: Dominance (D), Inducement (I), Submission (S), and Compliance (C).

The DiSC model provides a common language that people can use to better understand themselves and adapt their behaviors with others — within a work team, a sales relationship, a leadership position, or other relationships.

This website provides in-depth information about DiSC: https://www.discprofile.com/

Resilient Viruses:

There are things which will stay in our mind for quite a long time or even forever.

Idea: A new concept which is sprung into the mind and somehow you do not have a push to do it. This stays in the mind as a resilient virus and makes your mind restless. Whatever way you try to make it go away, this will keep pulling you to do something about it until a decision is made.

Unfinished Job: When you know a job you are supposed to finish is not fully done to your satisfaction (unless it is given full responsibility to others to handle), it is going to keep bothering you until you take time to finish it. All pending jobs also fall into this category.

Pain: Depending on what caused the pain, it might stay in the mind for a very long time. Over time, this can calm down, but the effect will continue throughout a whole lifetime. The only way to reduce its effect is to make yourself occupied by doing other things bigger than yourself.

Brain Power:

From the day we are born, all the experiences we have had are stored in the brain. The actions we have repeated, again and again, are easily accessible as though it is at our fingertips and we are able to perform those activities efficiently. The things we rarely have done fade over time from memory.

Whatever we do, it is stored in the form of neural connections. The more we repeat what we do, those connections become stronger. Stronger connections are recollected quickly, while feeble connections are not accessible and are forgotten. This exercise of memory muscle building is called **neuroplasticity**.

All new thoughts create connections. When repeated, these connections become stronger. The stronger you believe in something, the more it becomes your reality. Whether we like or do not like the thoughts, when repeated, connections are made stronger. The brain does not differentiate between good and bad connections. It stores everything to shape one's behavior.

The quest to conquer the brain is never attained.

"The human brain is a funny thing:
it's very susceptible to tempo and melody.
You put the right words to it, and it becomes very
influential."
-Ray Stevens

Neuroplasticity is at work throughout life. What we want to keep in our brain is completely our choice.

The power of a human brain is not confinable.
Rightly employing
such an infinitely powerful machine is smart.

Blame

The human mind is very peculiar in its behavior. If good, it takes credit. If things go wrong, it finds a person or a thing as a target to blame.

When you blame others for what happened, you are showcasing that you do NOT have any power to change.

Learning and growth happen only if you take responsibility and own up to your mistakes.

"You are not a failure until you start blaming others for your mistakes."
-John Wooden

Think about all the issues happening in our daily lives, small and big fights, misunderstandings, etc. Who should we blame?

Think about the issues we have in society – corruption, fighting, gun violence, etc. Who should we blame?

Blame Others or Take Responsibility. It is a Choice.

Instead of spending time and energy on blaming, try to come up with a solution to resolve the issue and put in procedures and practices, so that it won't happen again.

Art

Art is a diverse range of human activities, including creating visual, auditory or performing artifacts (artworks), expressing the author's imaginative, conceptual idea, or technical skill intended to be appreciated for their beauty or emotional power (Definition from Wikipedia).

Art satisfies the prime needs of the human being to achieve one's life purpose.

"The most beautiful thing we can experience is the mysterious. It is the source of all true art and science."
— Albert Einstein

Different art forms:

Visual art is a form of art that uses any medium to signify the artist's idea, sentiment, and imagination — visually. Examples of visual arts: paintings, drawings, sculptures, photography.

Performing art is the form of art which includes dance, music, opera, films, theater, drama, magic shows, and stand-up comedies. In modern-day, it is the most celebrated and appreciated form of art.

Literary art includes creative writing and literature such as poetry, books, and drama.

The world cannot be the way it is today without the innovations that have happened over the course of mankind's development. I categorize this under a new form of art called ***Innovation art.***

Innovation art is a special art skill, which continuously builds the world for the betterment, and, in turn, provides hope that everything is possible.

An artist with his/her artistic mind can imagine the future and communicate the solution for problems existing in real life.

As humans, we are all provided with an intellect to experience, to appreciate, and to create our own art.

All art is human created.

Through art, both the one who creates and the one who consumes/appreciates the beauty, can experience divinity.

Divine experience is Art.

As you start realizing the art form in everything, your life experience will be glorified.

Spend time on what you love, so that work won't feel like work, it becomes your Art.

"The art is long, life is short."
-Hippocrates

Work

During the pre-industrial and industrial times, people had to put in a lot of hard work to accomplish the things they wanted to do. While they were active, they had to spend all their time working hard to save for their retirement.

> ***"Work Hard, Rest Easy."*** *– was the golden slogan then.*

Now in the 21st century, even though hard work is essential, that is not the only ingredient for success and to have a fun filled life and enjoyable retirement. Even if you are working hard and are a good person, if you are not adapting to changes quickly enough, you won't be able to safeguard yourself from failure.

Smart work determines what to work, where to work, how to work, and to always adapt.

Smart work has to be combined with hard work to achieve success. At the same time, being smart but lazy to do the work is not going to take you anywhere.

Constantly innovate the way you work. Question yourself, is there a better way to do what I'm doing?

Identify the best way to get things done within the means of the current situation. Then, work towards achieving it.

Have a clear direction to reach the ideal best way. When you reach the ideal best, it is time to re-evaluate and find out the better and more ideal options. At every level, check if what you are doing is worth doing, or if it needs a pivot.

There is no one standard success formula – you need to innovate based on your interests. Use books, patterns, and practices as your tools to identify the things which will work for you. Focus your energy to achieve your prime needs.

Success is a journey and you need to continue your work without stopping. There is no defined limit for what a human can achieve, rather it is the mind that draws the limits.

When you know you need to do something and you have to do it at that time, but you delay it for later, it is called procrastination. When that becomes your behavior, you are deemed lazy and you are expected to fail.

Qualities of smart work:

- Make work as Art, so you love what you're doing.
- See problems as opportunities.
- Constantly innovate better ways to do what you are doing – be efficient.
- Employ the right resources for the appropriate type of work.

- Delegate work to maximize your time, but ensure it is delivered with quality.
- Finish the work in the stipulated time instead of always working late to accomplish it.
- Pivot as and when needed without hesitation to cut the waste.

At times, you need to do hard work, but always have a vision to do it better and in the best way by doing smart work.

Smart work is the lifestyle of hard work, perseverance, planning, and mainly self-discipline, which leads to building wealth.

Quote for the new era –

Work Smart, Relish Life.

Entrepreneurship

Entrepreneurship is about transforming the world by solving existing problems, which will create a direct or indirect benefit to the people and thereby generate profit.

Entrepreneurship – the modern day innovation breeding ground.

Entrepreneurship is what people do to take their career and dreams into their hands and lead it in the direction of their choice. It's about building a life on your own terms.

"You never change things by fighting the existing reality.
To change something, build a new model that makes the existing model obsolete."
— R. Buckminster Fuller

Multiplayer strategy game:

Have you ever played a strategy game such as "Age of Empires" or "Clash of Clans"?

The overall objective of these games is to build your empire, starting from the stone age and to keep upgrading to different ages until you reach a highly advanced technology age.

- You will start by collecting wood and meat to build facilities.
- Once you create people, you can start delegating the work to build more.
- You monitor them, so that they are doing what they are supposed to do.
- During this process, your opponents try to build similar empires and try to crush you.
- You need to fight back or you need to crush them before they act on you.
- You never stop growing, as you need to continue building to WIN.

Entrepreneurship follows a similar path as playing a strategy game – when you start, you may have to do all the work by yourself until you reach a point where you can hire resources to delegate the work. You need to constantly keep upgrading your empire and always be ahead of the competition.

Risk: Safe Job vs. Entrepreneurship

When the recession hit, people lost jobs.

When something got outdated, people lost jobs.

When there was a problem in management, people lost jobs.

When there was something not in direct control, people lost jobs.

There is no safe job, per se. As discussed in the topic "Money", if your investments are not diversified, you will suffer when the tough times hit.

The same is also applicable for entrepreneurship, if not managed properly.

Whether you work for someone or you run a business, your net result is to make money for the life that you always wanted.

If you are doing the job you really wanted to do, then it is a gift.

The biggest advantage of entrepreneurship is one can do what they want to do and choose what is the net result they want to achieve in terms of money, value, fame, etc.

Both have a benefit and a risk. You have to opt based on your needs.

"Why fit in when you were born to stand out?"
– Dr. Seuss

A risk is what you will lose when you fail.

Take time to really think about what your risk is. Then determine when is the right time to explore.

"Never test the depth of the river
with both the feet."
– Warren Buffet

Calculate your risk and determine what you can afford to lose so that you can take brave action. All businesses are always taking calculated risks.

When you are at an early age, this risk tends to be very small and it gets magnified as you grow in age. You always have the option to withstand multiple failures, if any, when you start to explore at an early age.

> **Building a safe anthill should not be your goal.**
> **Rather, building an empire should be.**

Entrepreneurship is an exploration.

Entrepreneurship is an experience.

Entrepreneurship is a necessity.

Entrepreneurship is to make a profit.

Entrepreneurship is fun.

What is the purpose of your life? Create and live an experience you want, or opt for a so-called "safe" job?

> **"Twenty years from now you will be**
> **more disappointed by the things that <u>you didn't do</u>**
> **than by the ones you did do.** **So throw off the**
> **bowlines. Sail away from the safe harbor.**
> **Catch the trade winds in your sails.**
> **Explore. Dream. Discover."**
> – Mark Twain

Key Ingredients

Five key ingredients of a successful entrepreneur are:

Motivation ~ Strategy ~ Execution ~ Value ~ Resources

Motivation: Passion & Purpose

When passion combines with strong purpose, employed to achieve your goal, it becomes the fuel for the long journey.

When the purpose is not supported in your heart, your journey is going to suffer.

At the same time, if your purpose is not your passion, it will not live for a long time.

Motivation = Passion x Purpose

Strategy: Areas to Focus

- Idea – how it will solve the problems now and in the future, and its direction it is headed
- Marketing – how to spread the word and make others buy in on the idea
- Sales – lead generation, lead maintenance, and converting a lead to a customer
- Maintenance – maintaining the existing customers, by keeping them close so that they don't look elsewhere
- Innovation – consistently bringing in new ideas for the betterment

- Managing employees – motivation, team building, individual growth
- Cash flow (Money) – very important vitamin for the organization. It needs to cover the cost of current running, future investment, profit, etc.
- Diversification to build resiliency, while maintaining core values
- Managing connections with people
- Managing infrastructure
- Government rules – tax, employment, federal, state and local laws, etc.
- Energy – building motivation and confidence, and always keeping it high.

All of the above are equally important to build and run a successful enterprise.

Initially, you as an individual or a small team needs to create and execute on the above strategies.

As you start growing, you need to identify the right resources to push higher into your success zone.

Execution:

Execution is a special skill which requires potential, perseverance, and action to reach the goal.

Giving up is easy.

Understand that the brain loves easy actions. We should resist giving up; we should always be aiming to achieve.

Commitment

While others seem to be spending time on external activities for fun, as an entrepreneur, you need to work on your vision for the future, which requires self-discipline and commitment.

Many times it is not just the individual commitment that is enough. You need to convince your close family and friends to understand your direction and have them provide continuous support.

Tomorrow's dreams are built on today's sacrifices.

Value:

Through products or services, you need to show value in order to be accepted as a provider. It is very important that each customer feels the service they received is worth the money they spent on it.

Customers do like to pay more when they are satisfied.

Word of mouth marketing is the only way to crack the virality code in business.

Virality = Value produced / Money (and/or) Time Invested (by users)

If you want to achieve a **"J"** growth curve, identify the elements in business which can make the customer realize value, so that they can go out of their way to promote your product/services.

Quality:

The success of your work is determined by the quality of your delivered product.

If it fails the quality test, it will never allow you to take off. If the quality is good initially, but it degrades over time, it can also bring down your whole enterprise.

> **"Customers don't measure you on how hard you tried, They measure you on what you deliver."**
> – Steve Jobs

Sometimes you need to trade the time and cost for quality. You need to cautiously make this decision since it will make or break your whole effort.

Resources:

People and Teamwork, Network, Technology, and **Money** are the key resources that should be employed in the right amounts to your advantage.

Out of all the above, technology plays a vital role in today's enterprises. When technology is exercised to its fullest, it can reduce the need for other resources.

For example, in today's age, if your business does not have an internet presence, it is missing out on a huge opportunity.

Qualities of an entrepreneur:

- Challenge the status quo.
- See opportunities in every encounter.
- Have a vision and a strategy to achieve, as well as periodically refining the strategy.
- Set new goals and push the limits to achieve.
- Focus on continuous innovation.
- Strive to crack the virality code.
- Do NOT accept "No" or "Not Possible" as an answer easily. Instead, explore.
- Always listen to the customers and bring in the changes to satisfy the customer's needs quickly.
  - Word of mouth promotion is more effective than any other means of marketing.
- Utilize resources effectively – Money, People, Network, and Technology.
- Maintain integrity with customers, employees, and other people in your connections.
- Be hopeful, patient, persistent, and always learn.
- Relentlessly cut waste.
- Don't procrastinate to pivot.

Responsibility:

Entrepreneurship is the ultimate responsibility.

- To the employees – whatever the outcome, you still need to ensure to pay their monthly salary and other business expenses
- To society
- To maintain credibility
- To yourself and your family

"Act so that the effects of your action are compatible with the permanence of genuine human life"
– Hans Jonas

Success and Failure

Failure is simply the opportunity to begin again, this time more intelligently.
– Henry Ford

What is Success?

- Is it achieving the highest college degree (doctorate)?
- Is it becoming the President or achieving any higher post in any organization?
- Is it earning lots of money?
- Is it a one-time achievement?

Each person has their own definition of what success means to them. It doesn't stop at achieving their first set goal. It always changes over time, and a new goal is set every time an old one is achieved.

Failures are the stepping stones for success:

Read the life histories of successful people to understand their journey, which will give you the necessary pointers, which can be very helpful during tough times.

Some of the great achievers you can explore are Walt Disney, Henry Ford, Thomas Edison, Oprah Winfrey, Steven Spielberg, Michael Jordan, Jack Ma, Albert Einstein, J.K. Rowling, etc.

Success is a journey and failures are the obstacles on the way.

"I have not failed. I've just found 10,000 ways that won't work"
– Thomas A Edison

When times are tough, you need to keep saying to yourself, "maybe I am just one more step away from seeing the glory to overcome the hurdle". Instead of sinking, explore the possibilities to handle.

You cannot achieve success or failure if you don't even take action in the first place.

Inaction = No Success and/or No Failure.

"Satisfaction lies in the effort, not in the attainment. Full effort is full victory."
— Mahatma Gandhi

New Normals

In human history, there are several great innovations our ancestors have made that continue to transform the world for the better, time after time. Now, we are here, having the better world to enjoy.

Visualize the world before each of the great innovations, how the world would have been, and how our ancestors spent their lives without them. This will help us to understand the life we are lucky to lead, as well as the responsibility that we have, to use these innovations wisely and make them better for the future generations.

The control of fire by the early humans was a huge transformer in human life as it provided warmth, protection, improvements in hunting, cooking, tool making, etc.

Can you think of the world without fire?

The wheel has revolutionized the way early human beings traveled and transported goods from one place to another. Earlier people or animals had to carry the goods or walk long distances. With wheels, the world changed forever, making everything go faster.

Can you think of the world without the wheel?

The invention of the school system to pass knowledge from one generation to the next?

The invention of electricity?

The invention of the light bulb?

The invention of television, cell phone etc.?

The innovations in transportation, science, medicine, technology, etc.?

Can you think of a world without all of the new normals?

The curiosity of our ancestors drove them to try different things. As a result, ideas sparked, which led to innovations and accidental discoveries, altogether transforming the world forever.

Humans are the only species that can do much bigger things than their physical capacity by employing their unique gift of the sixth sense.

We still have a lot of unresolved issues in spite of all these great innovations: terrorism, deadly diseases, psychological issues, ego fights, nuclear threats, hunger, education for all, clean water, global warming, pollution, extinction, etc.

What is your idea to change the world for good?

Moral Loan

Since the time we got the ticket to walk this world, we started to enjoy the services provided to us.

In this physical, materialistic world, **everything** has a cost.

Moral Loan: A loan borrowed without an obligation to return to the lender, and instead serve the world on a grand scale to feel content.

From the day we were born until we reached an age of maturity to take care of ourselves, we consumed several services from family, friends, teachers, strangers, and unknown sources to navigate the world without a legal binding to pay them back for those services.

Every mom has to take care of the baby in her womb until the baby gets delivered to the physical world successfully. The fun, the pain, and physical and mental sacrifice a mother goes through cannot be equated to the value. Every person born into this world is morally obligated to their mom without a doubt.

The schools we went to, roads we used, hospitals, parks, and places of worship are all human-created and most are used free of charge or at a very subsidized (reduced) cost. None of us creates all this from scratch to consume these services. What is the cost of all that we consumed?

If you really think along these lines, the pieces of advice and support we received, recommendations when we were not able to make choices, and motivations, all together helps in shaping the life we live and for the future. Each of us so tightly depends on each other at different levels.

The world seems like it is NOT obligated to give us anything.

Why were we given all this?

What is the motivation?

"If I have seen further it is by standing on the shoulders of Giants."
– Isaac Newton

Who sees further: a dwarf or a giant? Surely a giant, for his eyes are situated at a higher level than those of the dwarf. But if the dwarf is placed on the shoulders of the giant, who sees further? We learn from their wisdom and move beyond it.

We don't deny the shoulders of the giants. Are we not obligated?

We have to share air, water, and land without an option.

Can humans enjoy a real democracy from within and outside?

How can the violence and the pain caused to fellow beings all over the world be eradicated?

Do you realize we are obligated by a moral loan to give back as the need arises in order to be human?

Being thankful is one thing. On the other side, is something expected out of us? Are we bound by a "**Moral Loan**" to this society?

Every action we take needs to have a consideration of the impact it will produce in society, not just the profits of the individual or a group of individuals.

What can *YOU* do to make our generation and future generations enjoy the best life?

"Don't judge each day by the harvest you reap, but by the seeds you plant."
– Robert Louis Stevenson

SECTION 2 – PATTERNS & PRACTICES

Introduction – Patterns & Practices

"You cannot change your FUTURE, but you can change your HABITS. And surely your HABITS will change your FUTURE."

– APJ Abdul Kalam

The patterns and practices which are discussed in the forthcoming chapters are helpful to me and I can assure you that the time you invest in learning and practicing them will be worth it.

Even though the patterns and practices have a lot of potentials, I want to emphasize the importance of the principles at a higher level. Understanding the principles to the core can help you to invest the needed time on what is important for you.

"What you want" *is not* ***"what you expect"*** *But your* ***expectations*** *associated with the* ***actions you take*** *will result in your life experiences!!!*

To bring your expectations close to your wants, it requires sacrifice, work, focus, and pivots as and when necessary.

The patterns, and practices ahead will help you travel your journey gracefully.

The patterns and practices are organized into 5 categories:

- **Prime Growth Patterns**
  - Time Machine
  - Egg Hunt
  - Dream Projector
  - Desire to Destination: D2D marathon
- **Watchdog Patterns**
  - Border Wall
  - Carousel
  - Smart Assistant
  - Gauge and Grow
- **Driver Patterns**
  - Books
  - Quotes
- **Motivational Pattern** – Grand Finale
- **Simplified Yogic Practices** for the common man.

To practice the tools explained in this section, all you need is a notebook, a pen, and highlighters. You can also use a computer, but I recommend that you start with a notebook first. Once you master the patterns, you can opt for any device you like. When you write it down, it actually creates a different image in the brain, which helps to solidify your thoughts in a better way. It has been proven that handwriting something leads to better success in learning.

SECTION 2.1 – PRIME GROWTH PATTERNS

Time Machine

"The life of every man is a diary in which he means to write one story, and writes another, and his humblest hour is when he compares the volume as it is with what he vowed to make it."
– J.M. Barrie

Journaling generally involves the practice of keeping a diary or journal that explores thoughts and feelings surrounding the events of your life. There are several ways to do this. Many great achievers have practiced journaling.

I inherited this habit during my college days from my grandfather after I saw him writing diaries every day. I wrote for a few years, and then stopped after I finished college and moved on to work. About 15 years later, I came across an article on journaling and its benefits, and so I started jotting down my daily activities.

Instead of writing with lots of details, I started off by putting key notes in the form of a time log and started marking the things I valued in categories with different markers. By doing this, I also started noticing there were time slots where I didn't put any information.

Over the course of some time, it started revealing important things:

1. **Collective Intelligence** – I am precisely able to recollect on what I was doing by referring to the notes I had written previously.
2. **Black Holes** – In the initial days, there were many time slots where I wrote nothing and I questioned myself why. I realized that I was putting off the work, which I was supposed to do. Instead, I was wasting my time. This important revelation helped me make it a habit to log my activities more often. I consciously started doing this logging process every 30 minutes. After a few weeks of practice, I started seeing a huge improvement in time gain, and that was the biggest sense of achievement.
3. **Time Categories** – The highlighted areas of my log showed how productive I was on a daily/weekly basis and it gave me the urge to avoid the black holes of time.
4. **Trends & Behavior** – I created a measure on daily/weekly/monthly trends on how I spent my time to understand my interests.

This process of logging down important notes in an interval of 30 minutes to 1 hour provided me with collective intelligence over a long period of time, where I can quickly recollect my activities by taking a glance at my previous entries. Additionally, this process of journaling helped with the identification of the black holes which, in turn, helped me identify the distractors. Furthermore, by highlighting different categories with different colors, I discovered trends about my behavior. This process helped me rightly invest my time and plan for the future accordingly. This provided all the things a mystical "***Time Machine***" is said to give.

So, I started calling this practice, *"Time Machine"* and created two "Time Machines" for myself:

1. Office Time Machine
2. Personal Time Machine

Time Machine allows you to take control of your time and organizes the time needed for all the things that matter to you. It also helps you identify the distractors so you can use them moderately or completely avoid them.

Maintaining ***integrity*** with your "Time Machine" is a very important criterion.
It is going to reveal your true ***YOU***.

Pick a highlighter color for each time category. The time categories I used were:

*   Orange – new learning, creative/productive work
*   Pink – fun time – family time, games, hobbies etc.

- No highlight or nothing written – Black Hole – distractions, time on social media, casual browsing etc.

When a sculptor creates an elephant, each touch of the chisel shapes the stone. While carving an eye, he barely strikes the stone, but those light strokes are as vital as the rough shaping blows. There is no such thing as an unimportant blow.

Every time slot, small or big, matters;
Using it to your advantage matters.

Egg Hunt

*"You can't connect the dots looking forward;
you can only connect them looking backwards.
So you have to trust that the dots will somehow
connect in your future."*
- Steve Jobs

What is "thinking outside of the BOX"?

What is creativity?

What is connecting the dots?

To connect the dots, first, you need to see the dots.
But what is a dot?

There are lots of problems which are experienced
by people with or without them realizing it. A dot is a
discrete idea which solves a different problem in a
different situation. Once you know of their existence,
you can try connecting them to solve the puzzle you
have in hand.

Let's think about the invention of the airplane.
About a century ago, even though people were able to
travel locally, they were unable to cross an ocean or
travel long distances without taking a lot of time. Many
were put to the challenge of inventing the flying
machine which would allow people to reach their
destinations quickly. The Wright brothers were able to
solve the problem by connecting the concepts of how
birds fly using wings and how a motor can provide

acceleration as shown in vehicles. Soon, airplanes became a reality in our lives.

In today's world, the majority of people are using smartphones. Fifteen years ago, it was not in existence and people were using keypad phones to call others and were using computers to browse the internet. Apple came up with the first touch screen smartphone which allowed us to do both tasks in a small device. This transformed the whole world, in terms of how we do daily things.

In both instances, the innovators were successfully able to connect different solutions – **Dots** – which were solving problems in other areas.

An egg hunt is a game played on Easter day where decorated eggs (which may be chocolate eggs or artificial eggs containing candies) are hidden for children to find. When the hunt is over, prizes may be given for the most eggs collected, or for the largest or the smallest egg.

When little kids play this, they will have a burst of energy to collect lots and lots of eggs to become the winner. Only when they find an egg, they can collect it. The same thing is applicable to anybody who wants to solve problems. When they learn how different problems are getting solved with their respective solutions, they can try to connect these solutions to see whether they can solve the problem at hand.

Egg hunt is a quest to uncover dots.

With the abundance of information available to all of us through the internet, it is very easy to see a lot of dots. Google/Bing search, books, websites, blogs, and TED/ TEDx videos are some of the sources to uncover the dots. At the same time, there are also lots of distractions you must avoid in this dot hunting process.

If you hear the stories little kids create and tell, you can see how they connect unrelated things and tell a great story. As we grow, we are forgetting that we even possess that skill. If you keenly notice, it is our logical thinking that limits us by not allowing us to even experiment in our thoughts, thus restricting us from connecting the dots.

Like a little kid, while hunting for eggs during Easter, you should also hunt for dots whenever possible. This process makes your thinker muscles stronger. Once we start realizing how varied problems are solved using different disjoint solutions, the same process will help to connect the dots to solve the existing problems.

Egg hunting makes you creative, adaptable and always ready.

Dream Projector

Your first thought is rarely your best and final thought. It can be an ignitor for a big thing, but it always, always, requires tinkering to make it shine.

Dream Projector is a technique at your disposal to see whether that dream spark can become your desire and if it is worth pursuing.

Any spark of an idea which strikes you, which you can act upon to solve something, is an initial dream.

Once you realize that initial spark, write it down in a notebook, which I call a "***Dream Collector***". The next logical step is, for each dream, allocate a separate section of pages in the same notebook or identify an individual notebook which will be your "***Dream Projector***".

<u>Now it is time to think about your idea by asking many questions:</u>

Why do I want to pursue this?

What is the goal of this project?

What is it going to produce as direct and indirect benefits?

How do I do it?

What resources do I have? And so on.

The more questions you answer, the more likely you are to make the right decision.

The tools you can employ to project your dream are discussed below.

Mind Map –

A mind map is a diagram used to visually organize information. A mind map is hierarchical and shows relationships among pieces of the whole. This is a quick way to put our arms around the whole idea of what we want to achieve and reveals all the important pieces.

Major ideas are connected directly to the central concept, and other ideas branch out from them.

Mind maps can be drawn by hand, either as "rough notes" or as higher quality pictures utilizing any of the software drawing tools.

Impact mapping is a special kind of mind map. It is a strategic planning technique that can prevent organizations from getting lost while building products and delivering projects, by clearly communicating assumptions, helping teams align their activities with overall business objectives, and making better roadmap decisions.

Vision Board is any type of board on which you write text or display images that represent the vision of your life and what you want to become. Creating and using vision boards serves several purposes, most importantly: identifying your vision and giving it clarity, reinforcing your affirmations, and keeping your attention on your intentions.

If you want to start a business, use the template called ***Business Model Canvas*** – a very simple 1-page tool you can implement by using a pen and paper, which can help clarify your idea and also aid in identifying areas that you never thought about.

***Business Model Canvas* –**

The Business Model Canvas is a strategic management and lean startup template for developing new business models or documenting the existing ones. It is a visual chart with elements describing a firm's or product's value proposition, revenue streams, cost model, infrastructure, and target customers.

Once you get to some level of understanding on what you want to create, the product or service you want to offer, do apply the concept "Test the waters", before going in full blown. The most successfully adapted concept is to apply the ***Minimum Viable Product (MVP)*** on your idea.

Minimum Viable Product (MVP) is a development technique in which a new product or website is created with sufficient features to satisfy early users. The final, complete set of features is only designed and developed after considering feedback from the product's initial users.

Creating small MVPs and building on top of the initial MVP is similar to how honey bees go to several flowers and pick the nectar from each flower to build the honeycomb in small steps. A honeycomb can be used in any stage, big or small. At the initial stage, it is an MVP, and as it reaches its fullest size, it becomes a complete honeycomb.

By applying the tools above, one can get clarity on whether your dream can become a desire to pursue.

"You hit what you aim at, and if you aim at nothing you will hit it every time." – Zig Ziglar

The problem with *NOT following* the Dream Collector and Dream Projector is that we lose the precise thoughts we had during the initial moments and sometimes we may forget the idea in whole. If you cannot put in the time to think on the idea right away, then take some quick notes in whatever form possible so you can remind yourself at a later time to help with the projection process.

Sleep on the idea for a day or two and if all your thinker muscles are in alignment to take this dream to the next step, jump into action.

Desire to Destination – D2D Marathon

"Perseverance is more prevailing than violence; and many things which cannot be overcome when they are together, yields themselves up when taken little by little."

-Plutarch

When starting as a dream spark and becoming a strong desire in the heart, a destination is not the next immediate door simply available to open. It requires planning, execution, evaluation, feedback, improvement, and the cycle continues until the final goal is reached.

The very important step at this moment is to visualize the full vision of how it will be when achieved and identify the objectives that need to be met. With that being said, identify all the steps to be taken, to achieve each one of the objectives. The next step is to prioritize them and establish how to execute the important things first, and move to the next, one after another.

The grandeur vision or each objective should be split into achievable milestones. By achieving each milestone, it should result in achieving a bigger vision.

A very important factor which will determine the success of your journey from a desire to a destination is the **goal date.** If the goal date is not deterministic, it will show up as delays or poor quality deliveries or simply no movement and stay as a long, distant star that you are not capable of achieving.

Once the milestones are prioritized, setting the goal dates for each milestone is a must, as this will provide the drive needed to achieve each of them within the specified deadline.

"A goal without <u>a date</u> is just a dream."
– Milton H. Erickson

Demonize Deadline:

Fear can be a catalyst for action and to retain focus.

We all know that when we achieve goals, they reap benefits, but in spite of the good things, it is a natural tendency to procrastinate to do the needed action and wait until the last moment hits.

We do know it is important, that's why we set a goal date. But since the mind likes fun over pain, it tries to avoid work.

To avoid procrastination and rushing at the last moment or to avoid delay, you need to portray a demonized future self of you, not achieving the goal, and also visualize the loss in opportunity and the damage it might bring.

When the fear of not achieving is bigger, it will push you to do the action and help you to finish it before the expected time.

Desire to Destiny (D2D) Marathon:

I have used "Scrum" as a <u>base process vehicle</u> to formulate this pattern.

What is Scrum? Scrum is an iterative and incremental framework for managing product development.

Scrum is used in a variety of fields to achieve success, especially in professional setups. It is time for us to adopt and apply the proven techniques in our dream projects to increase our chances of success. It is a formalized commonsense practice.

I have adapted the Scrum process in the below-prescribed form, which I call **Desire to Destination Marathon (D2D Marathon).**

If you want to expand your understanding of Scrum, there are several books and websites to explain the concept.

<u>D2D Marathon follows a five-step process from a very high level</u>

- ➢ Pre-Start - Step 0: Dream Projector – Now you have a strong desire to execute
- ➢ Step 1: Create Backlog list
- ➢ Step 2: Prioritize the items and create multiple quarterly release plans (as needed)

➢ Step 3: Execute the first quarter release plan
- Validate your output
- Celebrate your release completion.

➢ Step 4: Continue to your next release plan, repeat steps 2, 3, 4 until the final goal is achieved.

➢ Step 5: Publish your Art! Have Fun.

Backlog creation:

Once you convert your dream to a desire using Dream Projector, you need to finalize a list of things to be handled. Scrum calls this a backlog list.

Once the backlog list is created, prioritize the items which are more important to do and create an order of execution. Concentrate only on the items which you need to handle for the next few weeks. You don't need to make any detailed plans for the items which you are going to do next month or later, but always have a grander vision of how all these things need to flow.

The biggest power of Scrum is that the initial backlog list is not written in stone, it may change during the execution, and Scrum allows us to inspect it often and do necessary pivots as needed.

Release Plan:

Every project takes time. Sometimes it takes months or years. Instead of trying to achieve the whole chunk in a single shot, split your vision into manageable milestones and prioritize them to be executed in repeated cycles of timeboxes called release.

Every release plan should not exceed a maximum time period of 1 quarter (3 months). Some follow monthly release plans. It is based on your choice. My recommendation would be to keep a quarterly cycle.

Each Release Plan execution follows a five-step process

- ➢ Step 1: Create a weekly execution plan from your backlog list based on the priority.
- ➢ Step 2: Execute Tiny Execution – 1-week sprint
  - Inside each weekly sprint, perform work to finish the planned items.
  - Follow Time Machine and Egg Hunt regularly
  - At the end of the week, reflect on how and what you executed.
    - If all good, follow the same step in the upcoming Tiny execution.
    - If changes are required,– do the necessary modifications before proceeding.
- ➢ Step 3: Repeat the Tiny executions until the end of the quarter or till the release plan achievement, whichever comes first
- ➢ Step 4: Validate your output and direction
  - If the direction is good continue
  - Direction not good
    - If correction is needed, do a pivot

- If not worth continuing – STOP the waste.
➢ Step 5: Celebrate your release completion.

Tiny Execution – 1-week Sprint:

Any great work requires perseverance and if executed one step at a time, the culmination of small steps will reveal itself as a masterpiece.

Once the release plan is devised, now you have a quarterly goal to achieve. Reaching the goal requires action. Each tiny execution is timed to be a maximum of a 1-week sprint cycle. It can start on Monday and end at the weekend.

From the release plan, based on the priority, pick the most important items first. Ensure that each item or a combination of multiple items is able to be completed within the time frame of 1 week. If you think the particular item is going to take more than 1 week, split the items into multiple small items and prioritize them in order and take it into the 1-week sprint for execution.

Use Time Machine to log your work often and to ensure that you are able to achieve what you want on a daily basis.

Every day's success will lend itself to a weekly sprint success.

Reminders: Use some form of visual reminder which can motivate you to take action towards your goal. I use *Aspirant Tribal Bands* as a way to remind me to work towards my goal.

Sunday Reflection, Course Correction, Celebration:

Sunday is considered the first day of the week and can also be the day to reflect on the ART you created in the Tiny Execution for the past week.

Identify:

- What went well, which you are going to continue to do
- What went wrong, and what you need to change
- What new strategies you want to follow in the upcoming Tiny Executions
- If the course is correct, or if it needs pivoting

Celebrate what you are able to achieve and plan for the items to be handled for the next Tiny Execution.

Repeat the Tiny Execution cycles within the release period to achieve your release plan goals. Repeat your release plan again and again, until you achieve the final destination you put forth for yourself.

End of every release you should validate your direction and ensure you are in the right path, if you are not in the right direction, you need to do the necessary pivot (course correction) and proceed with the next release plan execution. During this if you determine, it is not worth continuing you should have the courage to stop the waste.

Every day's success will lend itself to a weekly sprint success.
Every successful sprint is one step closer to achieving your destination.

SECTION 2.2 – WATCHDOG PATTERNS

Border Wall

Everything in the universe has a border wall.

The sun and the planets in our solar system each have their own border wall called the atmosphere. Earth's atmosphere protects life on Earth by creating pressure allowing for liquid water to exist on its surface, absorbing ultraviolet radiations which are harmful to the living organism when they are exposed directly, warming the surface through heat retention, and reducing temperature extremes.

Every country has a border wall to defend itself from foreign intrusions, impose duties on imported goods, and control immigration and emigration.

Like the atmosphere does to the Earth, the skin acts as a barrier that protects the body from harmful things such as germs, toxic substances, etc. Additionally, it helps to regulate body temperature.

The upper and lower eyelids that can cover the eyes act as a border wall from foreign objects, such as, wind, dust, insects and bright light.

With a gazillion things happening around us every moment, it is very easy to get distracted and spend our time with no purpose. The brain prefers fun and familiar stuff over needed work and unfamiliar challenges. It is very easy to get sucked into quicksands of distractions laid around us.

A strong border wall is a need to protect yourself from the invasions of distractions.

The border wall is crucial to have, but a clear definition of what it is going to protect is equally or even more important as well.

What is it protecting? It is your **value system.**

Your personal value system can be defined by answering some of the questions below:

- What are the things I really want?
- Why do I want it?
- How much attention should I be giving to each item?
- Where should I be spending my time?
- What do I need to achieve in a week/month/quarter/year? and so on...

Add your own questions to clearly define your value system.

Check Post: Every time you encounter an activity, determine if it is a foreign invasion (distractions) or a needed item for you to take. Do not accept anything which will affect your value system or is not useful to your life.

If it is a needed item, determine whether it has to be done now or if it can wait. If it can wait, add it to your to-do list for later evaluation.

To avoid a drain of time and energy, you need to ensure you build a strong enforcement officer, the **Mind**, to protect your own value system. Also, define your past and current distractions. Time Machine can help in revealing the distractions so that you can devise a plan to mitigate it.

The **To-do list, Check Post,** and a **strong Mind** together will form a personal border wall to protect your value system.

Watch out for the time stealers.

How efficiently you can achieve what you desire is determined by your fortified border wall.

Carousel

A merry-go-round, also known as carousel is a large, rotating, entertainment ride at fairs, with wooden or plastic animals, on which children ride.

Carousels look very attractive, elegant and majestic. Kids love to go on this ride again and again. No
matter the number of times they go to the fair, they still want to take a ride on the carousel.

Everybody has their own routines in their life. Some routines are fun and some are a hassle to do. Review every routine that you are doing, or wanting to do, and see how you can make it fun. Like how every wooden or plastic animal in a carousel is important, ensure the activities you have are needed. Make those activities fun and attractive so that you don't fall behind or avoid them altogether.

Create your own routine carousels.

- Daily carousel
- Weekly carousel
- Monthly carousel
- Quarterly carousel
- Yearly carousel

Defining the carousel takes the stress away from remembering what you should be doing periodically without fail. This is one of the very important steps you should take in achieving what you want.

Periodic, routine carousels are also part of your value system, which should be protected by the "Border Wall" discussed in the last chapter.

Ensure that Time Machine has a log entry for every work activity in the carousel as it is being done.

Carousels will help you to be more organized.

Smart Assistants

With the advent of smartphones, technology has become a daily consumable for most people. With a calculator, calendar, messaging tools, social media, maps with GPS, and internet search engines, the smartphone aids in making our lives more comfortable.

We have apps for everything we need today. Choosing the right one is a challenge we face today.

Although technology makes things easier, it is also putting a dent on the individual's social relationships by creating a self-centric, isolated world.

Technology is a real enabler. We can find solutions to several problems, but there is also a problem when there are too many solutions to a single problem, which sometimes makes technology a hindrance rather than an enabler.

When we are stuck in an unknown territory and don't have a direction to go, collective human intelligence is the only way to seek a solution.

Whatever your life goals are, or whatever the problem you are stuck on, try to find people, who can mentor and assist you to overcome the obstacle quicker.

"You are the average of the five people you spend the most time with." -Jim Rohn

To create a chain of assistance, look at the number of people you are interacting with and divide them into three groups.

- One-third of them are people who more or less are at the same level as you, who you can discuss and socialize with.
- The second-third are the people who have achieved ten-fold compared to you. While it may be intimidating to go with them, they have already gone through the same roadmap which you want to travel, and they will be happy to share their experiences, which can help you.
- The last one-third are the people who are looking at you for your guidance, and by helping them, you can feel content.

People are the real smart assistants that you can count on to achieve success. Giving and taking is the secret sauce of life to make life the fullest.

Gauge and Grow

Measuring things started way before we all can even comprehend. It traces back to the 3rd or 4th millennium BC. Even the very earliest civilizations needed measurement for agriculture, construction, and trade purposes. Starting in the 18th century, modernized, simplified and uniform systems of weights and measures were developed, with the fundamental units defined by more precise methods in the science of metrology. The discovery and application of electricity were one factor motivating the development of standardized applicable units internationally.

We see measurements everywhere in our life. Time, money, and life quality and quantity are all measured and ranked against some kind of baseline for us to achieve and improve upon. This brings us to an important realization that if you don't measure what you do, you cannot make it better.

The theory of constraints (TOC), Scrum, Kanban, and LEAN are other popular processes applied today as very strong roots in measuring the quantity and quality of the work getting produced to improve the overall efficiencies.

The tools we described can be used with or without measuring the progress we made. But by measuring, it will provide you with the current position to understand if you are on the right track, or if you need to pivot and drive yourself towards your end goal.

Measuring and charting over a period of time will reveal our trends and behaviors. The insights you get from these will provide pointers to the immense potential waiting to be unlocked.

<u>Time Machine</u> – Measure your time investments in new learning, productivity, fun, and distractions.

<u>Egg Hunt</u> – Measure the number of dots and the number of connections you make on a weekly basis.

<u>Dream Projector</u> – Measure the number of dreams you captured and how many became desires to pursue.

<u>D2D Marathon </u>– Measure how much progress you are making every week and make an estimate of how much time it will take to achieve your success.

<u>Yogic Practices</u> – Measure your consistencies on how you performed daily practices.

Measure what matters to you.

SECTION 2.3 – DRIVER PATTERNS

Books

*"There is more treasure in books than in all the
pirate's loot on Treasure Island."*

– Walt Disney

A library or a bookstore is a modern day Treasure Island. One can paint their own future by getting inspired by reading books of their interest. One can really see how many genres are available and a good library will carry various books, which you will not be able to access through the internet.

**A library or a bookstore is a
modern day Treasure Island.**

Books are your <u>vital change agents,</u> which can provide the collective wisdom of the author in a very distilled form.

Books provide guidance and techniques which have worked for others and took them years to experiment, master and achieve. Their knowledge is available at a very affordable cost and is easy to be read in a week or two.

Studies show that many successful people in different fields have a habit of reading a variety of books and on average, they read 40 to 60 books a year, which is almost a book per week.

If you dream to reach a successful level, this is one of the skills you need to acquire as well.

Books expand your understanding and make you take BOLD steps.

In my opinion, books are a great way to spend time productively, and also if you were to give a gift, especially to the budding generation, gift them with great books. Books are priceless, and the change they can produce is intangible.

> **Every book is a thought seed.**
> **Each book's worth is intangible.**

When we want to give a gift to others, most times we are tempted to give material gifts for many reasons. Instead, always try to sneak in a book with your gift. This is an indirect way to empower them without the receiver knowing it.

One of the biggest secrets of rich people is, they spend money to make more money.

Nowadays, we have credit cards and spend a lot of money, and as a byproduct, we acquire spending points. How do you best use the points and make the most returns out of your points investment?

In my opinion, you can invest those purchase points in buying books. I use my Amazon credit card and with all the purchases I make, I get points, and I am able to buy a good number of books every year.

Convert your daily spending to a thought seed of growth.

Now Amazon also makes it easy to buy used books and rent books – what a great option for casual readers like me to utilize the points. One thing though, Amazon does not allow points to be used for Kindle reader books.

Quotes

In the great Indian epic of Mahabharata, there is a short story about the forest tribal chief's son Eklavya. He belongs to a family of hunters. He wanted to learn the art of archery to become a great archer. So, he asked his father to help him become one by getting training from the sage Guru Dronacharya.

During this period, schools were very different from the current age. They were called *gurukuls* (residential school), where students lived and got all kinds of education from the guru. Some of the education such as archery and war science was limited only to the royal family children.

Eklavya, who wanted to learn archery, requested the Guru Dronacharya to accept him as his disciple, so that he can also learn the skill. But Guru Dronacharya declined the boy by saying, "As per the Vedic caste system I cannot teach you."

The innocent tribal boy was deeply hurt because of this unfair system, which restricted him from learning the skill. He left the place with a broken heart but was still determined to learn archery.

After reaching his own forest, he made a statue of Guru Dronacharya in a secluded area and faithfully believed he practiced before his guru. Day after day, he took his bow and arrow, worshipped the statue of Guru Dronacharya, and started practice. In time, <u>faith,</u>

<u>courage, and perseverance transformed</u> him into an extraordinary archer.

Even though the story unfolds differently to show the respect of students to teachers, Eklavya is still praised as a great archer, and as a loyal and brave student in the epic of the Mahabharata.

Will power can overcome the shortcomings.

You will be lucky to have 1 role model who has all the qualities which you can simply follow. With the ever so busy world, searching for a role model itself is a Herculean task.

The wisdom packed inside a small capsule of a few lines in the form of a *quote* can provide the strength for the long journey ahead.

In this modern age, I believe that quotes can be our guiding principles which can act as role models for life.

A quote can be a virtual Guru.

My virtual gurus:

- Swami Vivekananda – famous spiritual leader of India – "Arise, Awake, and stop not till the goal is reached"
- Dr. A.P.J. Abdul Kalam – was an Indian Scientist and 11th president of India – "Everything starts with a dream, don't wait to sleep to start dreaming."

- His greatest works – Ignited Minds, Wings of Fire
- Satya Nadella – Microsoft CEO, – "Our industry doesn't respect tradition, it respects innovation".
- Many of the quotes I mentioned in this book collectively act as my virtual role model by driving my energy system and motivating me to achieve higher.

Quotes can be your virtual role models.

SECTION 2.4 – MOTIVATIONAL PATTERN

Grand Finale

How many days do you really celebrate in a year? Normally, we use 10% or 5% of the days for vacation, but do we ever really take time to celebrate our actions? If so, what percentage is that?

Often, we aren't even aware of where we are – so really we are lost. When lost, we fall prey to the states of delay, doubt, and confusion. Reflection always improves clarity because it changes perspective.

A celebration is a confrontation, giving attention to the transcendent meaning of one's actions. It is all about feeling proud of the actions performed and re-energizing for the journey ahead.

A celebration is self-acknowledgment and recognition for successfully completing every small step.

Grand Finale: Create a practice of taking stock of all the projects you are working on, and review the progress made in each of them. During this time of stock-taking, if we do realize we are not making progress on a project, we should pivot or cut the waste by not doing it. Combine this process with a celebration, so that you will be looking forward to doing this.

Cultivate a habit of doing this celebration periodically and call it your "Grand Finale".

Doing it periodically at regular intervals will provide a timebox, which is a great way to measure your progress.

My recommendation would be to do this "Grand Finale" on a quarterly basis.

<u>*Perform the following things:*</u>

1. Review the progress made towards each objective you have.
   - ➤ If things don't go well, do a pivot or stop.
2. Plan the objectives for the upcoming period.
3. Celebrate within your means.
   - ➤ Do something memorable which can help boost your energy and allow you to look forward to achieving the objectives you put-forth.
4. Feel proud of what you accomplished. Be thankful to all those who contributed to the achievement of your objectives.

Simplified Yogic Practices for a Common Man

Have you ever wondered what is the one and only thing which always remains with you throughout your whole life? It is your **body**.

To achieve something big in your life and enjoy its fruits, you need a <u>healthy body</u> and a good <u>control of your mind</u>. When one of these lags, it will show up in the outcome as a delay, unfinished job, or poor quality of life.

A sound soul <u>dwells</u> within a sound mind and a sound body.

Discussed below are some of the practices preached by yogis, and are practiced by several successful people to achieve their goals. I have provided them in a simplified form so that it can be followed
easily.

Rise Early for Your Passion

Get your extra hours by rising early, 4 AM is a good start. Try not to have any disturbance from any external sources during this time. Use this time for anything you want to achieve and for creating your *ART*.

I was a late riser for a long time, when I realized that I needed extra time and I could not skip anything I do on a regular day such as office work, time with family and friends, etc. The only way I could get more time is by rising early or staying awake late in the night. If you stay late and do work, since it is the end of the day, your best energy is already consumed for previous activities and your body is physically tired.

If you want to forcibly wake up because others told you, then you will be back into the trap of not being able to carry through forever.

You will wake up for sure, when you know you want time to yourself and you are going to spend that time on your passion or your dream.

DO NOT use phone/social media as soon as you wake up and also during this early morning time all extras can wait.

We definitely have time for those activites later in the day. Nothing is going to change by immediately looking at social media and becoming reactive and responding to others. Say NO to email checking also, it can definitely wait.

Drinking a glass or two of water can help hydrate and clean your gut easily.

"The early bird catches the worm"

Waking up early provides you with extra time boost than the rest who do not rise early. Waking up

116

early alone, is not enough, you also need to work towards catching the worms you want. By waking up early, you now have an advantage.

Vibrant Colors of Life

How many times have you gotten the opportunity to watch a sunrise or sunset? Every minute of the sunrise is different and every day is different. You can notice the change in colors in the sky, from black to light blue. During this progression, you can see the different smooth gradients of orange, red, pink, purple, etc. Along with the sunrise, when you experience the soft chill breeze, the melody of chirping birds, animal sounds, and the waves of the ocean or river, you can realize the immense power of nature and its gift to us. Even though you can try to capture it through a camera, what you can experience when watching while it is happening at the moment, cannot be equated to watching a video later.

You can realize the universe is changing every second while watching the sunrise/sunset, and you will never get the same instance again.

The universe is always changing and doesn't stop. One must embrace continuous changes in their life to be nimble.

Meditation

Meditation is a type of practice which helps you live in the present moment and not to delve into the past or future.

Many research studies have shown that meditation has various benefits in maintaining mental stability and curing diseases. Meditation works to balance the left and right hemispheres of the brain and creates harmony.

Meditation is the key to unlocking your untapped, limitless potential.

Meditation can be practiced anytime, by sitting upright, closing your eyes and by concentrating on your inhale and exhale process.

There are several types of meditation practices in use, to name a few, The Art of Living, Mindfulness, etc. You can try one or more and whichever suits your likings, you can follow.

Sound Body

Fifty years ago, there was more playing and doing hard work, so there was not an extra need to talk specifically about exercise. Even during those times, different forms of exercises were practiced to keep the body and mind fit.

Now, with so many advancements, things are becoming easy and readily available every day. Getting out often or practicing daily exercise routines   has become a luxury. We all know exercises are good, but we don't practice them regularly.

With so many priorities, there is a need for an easily doable practice which can be performed by all in a short time at any place with no cost.

5 Minutes – Strengthen Articulation

Notice all the joints in your body from top to bottom – jaw, neck, shoulder, elbow, wrist, finger, back spine, hip, knee, ankle, and toe.

Give each joint a quick rotation 10 times in a clockwise and counterclockwise direction.

15 Minutes – Sun Salutation

Surya Namaskar, the Sun Salutation, is a series of 12 postures performed in a single, graceful flow. Each movement is coordinated with your breathing. Inhale as you extend or stretch, and exhale as you fold or contract. Sun Salutation builds strength and increases flexibility.

Many YouTube videos and websites explain the steps of performing Sun Salutation. It gives a workout to the whole body.

When you perform one Sun Salutation, start with the right leg and for the next sequence, the left leg. Repeat this 12 times. It may take 15 minutes at most to finish.

As you grow older, your priorities change and the time for physical activities get squeezed. Spending 20 minutes on the above-stated practices can give the daily needed exercise, when you don't find time to do long physical workouts.

Playing a Sport

It's always fun playing a sport, whether it is an individual or group sport. This will keep your heart healthy, strengthen muscles, and keep the brain active. Try playing different sports to learn their rules and at the same time keep yourself healthy.

Fuel

Food and water are the fuel for our body. Our body absorbs minerals, vitamins, carbohydrates, and proteins from the food we eat and makes energy for us to move and perform actions, which strengthens our body and fights against infections.

We have more awareness of gadgets such as television, cell phones, gaming devices, etc. However, we are not spending the time to understand the functions of our own human body, and are taking things for granted until we face a health issue.

Did you know digestion starts from your mouth? When you eat, if you are not hungry or if your attention is on the TV or cellphone (basically, when your focus is not on eating food), your body doesn't produce the needed saliva to help digest the food. Gulping the food without chewing it not only puts a burden on your stomach, but also causes the food to go to waste without utilizing the minerals.

Our senses are the feedback systems of the body, which provide critical information on whether to intake food or not, and in addition with your knowledge, you should pick and choose the right food for you to consume.

What you intake makes you.

Your body is your choice, so make conscious choices to help yourself enjoy a healthy life for 100 plus years.

Sleep to Rejuvenate

When you had a good night's sleep or even a short nap during the day, you feel very refreshed after that rest. When you don't get a good night's sleep, the next day doesn't go well, as we feel sluggish and not motivated to do any work.

When we are awake, the brain is busy providing continuous instructions to all parts of the body so that all of them can perform their functions.

The brain needs lots of energy to continuously monitor and provide instructions. Because of this, the brain is designed not to spend energy to clean up the waste that is getting produced during the time we are awake. When we sleep, the brain can safely shut down some of the functions and spend energy on draining the waste out of the brain.

When all the waste is drained, we feel very refreshed when we wake up after a good sleep.

Empower Others

Each of us possesses some skills, which many others are in need of, to learn and advance their life.

When you realize the knowledge and work you provide to others are making a difference, it provides joy and fulfillment in your life.

Empower others to uplift you.

Happiness Farming

Many times we run for things that we don't have, not realizing the things we already possess, and always keep worrying about what is missing. Instead of worrying, work towards achieving the same.

Spend some time at the end of each day to be thankful for the good things that happened to you and the gift of the life you are able to lead. There could be worse things happening all around the world and you could have been a victim.

This daily practice of feeling grateful for what you possess is the process of happiness farming, which can shape your future for much more content and happy life. You may falsely perceive others control your happiness until you realize your part.

You are responsible for your happiness.

SECTION 3 – APPLICATION OF THE PATTERNS AND PRACTICES

Part 1 - A Journey – "The Making of: The modern You – Uncover P3"

Walt Disney's Four C's

"Somehow I can't believe that there are any heights that can't be scaled by a man who knows the secret of making his dreams come true. This special secret, it seems to me, can be summarized in four C's.
They are **curiosity, confidence, courage,** and **constancy**, and the greatest of these is **<u>confidence</u>**. When you believe in a thing, believe in it all the way."
– Walt Disney

Purpose:

To showcase:

1. How consistent small progressions made over a period of time can make a huge difference in achieving a mountainous goal.
2. How the application of patterns helped me in achieving the dream of writing a book.
3. How Time Machine helped to recollect the finer details of the past and helped me to keep on track.
4. How technology is an enabler.
5. The process of publishing a book and making it accessible to all.

Part 1 – Inception, Tiny Executions, MVP:1 Release

Before practicing the patterns, like many, when I got dream sparks, I'd think on them but didn't take any action most of the time, or at times I'd try to do some work towards the idea. However, the desire dies down and I would tend to fall back into inaction after a few days, and continue on with regular activities without pursuing the dream.

In 2007, I started working on a book but after writing a few pages, I stopped working on it.

For almost 10 years, deep inside, I had this unrealized dream as a resilient virus, but I didn't know where to begin.

In mid-2017, I started to invest time in reading a good number of books and watching many TED talks and motivational videos. From those, I got several pointers and with my experience working in the technology industry for about 18 years, I put together a set of patterns which I have explained in this book under Section 2, and started practicing them in my day-to-day life and began to reap positive results.

Pictorial Representation:

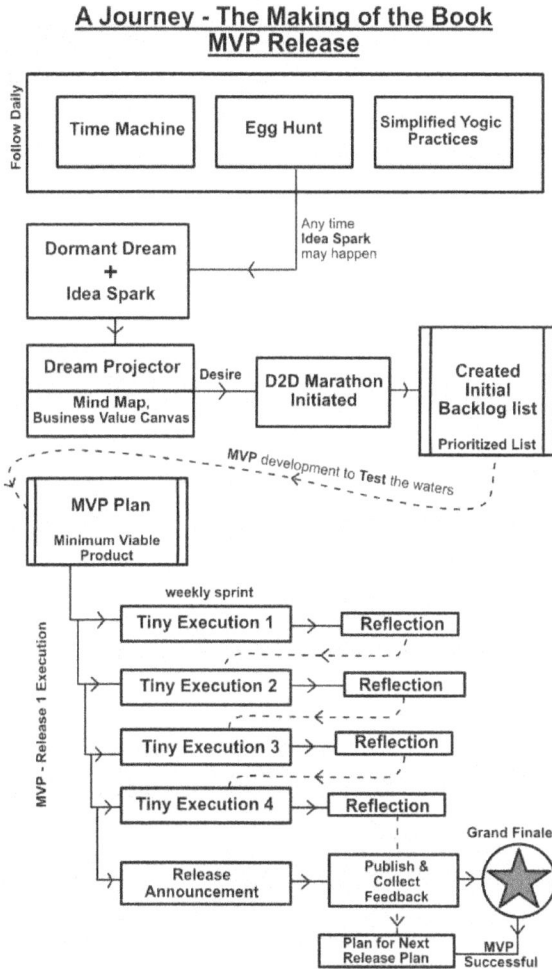

A Journey - The Making of the Book
MVP Release

Follow Daily
- Time Machine
- Egg Hunt
- Simplified Yogic Practices

Any time
Idea Spark
may happen

**Dormant Dream
+
Idea Spark**

Dream Projector
Mind Map,
Business Value Canvas

Desire

**D2D Marathon
Initiated**

**Created
Initial
Backlog list**

Prioritized List

MVP development to Test the waters

MVP Plan
Minimum Viable
Product

weekly sprint

MVP - Release 1 Execution

- Tiny Execution 1 → Reflection
- Tiny Execution 2 → Reflection
- Tiny Execution 3 → Reflection
- Tiny Execution 4 → Reflection
- Release Announcement

Publish & Collect Feedback

Grand Finale

Plan for Next Release Plan

MVP Successful

Refer Section 2, to understand the patterns such as Time Machine, Egg Hunt, Dream Projector, D2D Marathon, and Grand Finale.

Application of the patterns in the making of this book is as follows:

Three important things I continued to follow throughout the whole period of making of this book, which helped me to keep the momentum and drove me to completion are:

1.   Yogic Practices
2.   Time Machine
3.   Egg Hunt

Yogic Practices – Raise Up Early, Articulation & Sun Salutation:

When I had most of my time booked for activities, I wondered how I could get more time? My options were to stay late or rise up early. It was apparent that rising up early was the best choice because it could provide a fresh start and time for some exercise.

Initially, I was wasting time by looking at emails and social media, which ate up all of my early morning time, and I still wasn't doing what I actually wanted to do. I realized that if I didn't stop the distractions, I will never be able to do any work towards my goal.

By waking up between 4:30 and 5:00 AM, I was able to gain an extra 2 hours of time that I didn't have before. By forcing myself not to think about any other activities, I was able to focus just on the goal and had the creative juices flowing.

When you want to do work that you are passionate about, you will be able to wake up early.

Routines –

- Drink a cup or two of water (to clean up the gut).
- Do exercise – strengthen articulation (each body joint rotation), Sun Salutation (12 times)
  - Provides warmup and full body exercise in 20 minutes.

After that, I normally have time for about one and a half hours until 6:30 AM to work on the passion I want to pursue, like writing this book, creating materials for Headstream (DreamBigBuddy – coding club), etc.

Then I continue with the normal daily routines. This way, I don't have to steal time from family and other fun activities in the evening or weekends.

Time Machine:

I started logging notes of what I did every day. They consisted of the start and end time, and I even began highlighting the things I liked most. Initially, I was less productive in utilizing my time, but over time by identifying and fixing the time drains, I was able to increase my productive/creative work.

Time Machine also helped me go back and recollect what I was doing in the past and also helped me increase my productivity gradually, to a much higher level.

Self-time accounting will reveal behaviors about youself and provide you the opportunity to correct yourself at your own pace and style.

Time Machine is the base tool for all the things which one can employ to achieve anything.

Egg Hunt:

When you have a desire to do something, but don't know where to start, the first thing you can do is to explore things with whatever means you have and try to understand your strengths and find out where your talents are in need. There are several ways one can start the exploration. The path I took was to watching TED Talks videos regularly during the evening, while running on the treadmill.

Every day I watched different topics which provided awareness on different things - personality development, body, health, wealth, science, religion, etc.

On April 27th 2018, I came across a TED Talks video, "Ending The Old Boy Network: The New World of Publishing" by Andy Weir. This immediately inspired me to pick up one of my resilient viruses that had scratched my brain for a long time.

An idea sparked – I should write a book about what I am dreaming and set up a website on the things I have been practicing, which would definitely help others.

Inception
Dormant Dream to Desire – Dream Projector:

Anytime I get an idea spark or something similar, I jot it down in a notebook.

I expand on the spark by using these steps:

1. Define the intent and scope.
2. Find what I know and use it to my advantage.
3. Find what I don't know and how to get it.

The first tool I employed is a "**mind map**", which can quickly reveal the big picture and help collect and expand on the base idea.

Mind map of "The Modern You – Uncover P3"

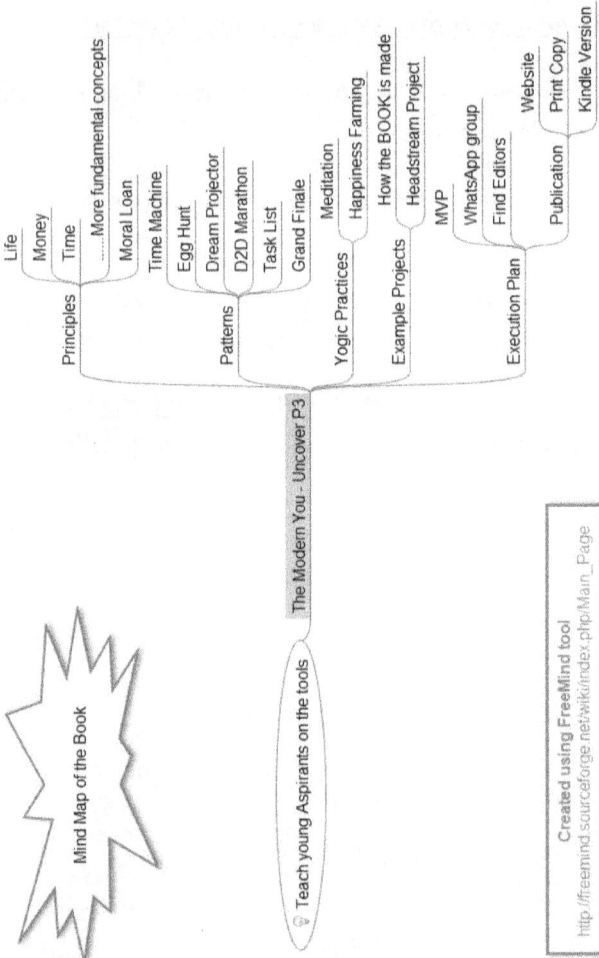

Mind Map of the Book

The Modern You - Uncover P3

Teach young Aspirants on the tools

Principles
- Life
- Money
- Time
  - More fundamental concepts
  - Moral Loan
  - Time Machine

Patterns
- Egg Hunt
- Dream Projector
- D2D Marathon
- Task List
- Grand Finale

Yogic Practices
- Meditation
- Happiness Farming

Example Projects
- How the BOOK is made
- Headstream Project

Execution Plan
- MVP
- WhatsApp group
- Find Editors
- Publication
  - Website
  - Print Copy
  - Kindle Version

Created using FreeMind tool
http://freemind.sourceforge.net/wiki/index.php/Main_Page

I also utilized the Business Value Canvas template in order to define the available resources, target audience, how to market at a very minimal cost, and the roadmap for the future.

The next important step is defining the scope of a ***Minimum Viable Product*** (MVP) of the book to validate the idea. Instead of just talking about the idea to others, making an MVP would get more traction and also help to get great feedback. Based on the feedback, I can build the next level of the project or sometimes even do a pivot, which can be a decision to continue or even drop the idea and do something else instead.

Steps to finish my first MVP:

1. Think of a name for the book which I want to write.
2. Finish a few anchor chapters which convey the intent and create curiosity.
3. Host it on a website, so I can share it easily and continue to add more.
4. Identify the reviewers who can help and provide feedback.

An MVP is not something written in stone. It can be changed as time progresses, but having a high-level boundary is needed to clearly see the goal post.

Initial Backlog List to Complete the Book, Created Utilizing the "Dream Projector":

- Write the book introduction
- Write the chapters in Section 1 – Principles – 10 chapters
- Write the chapters in Section 2 – Patterns – 8 chapters
- Write the closing
- Edit the book
- Design the front and back cover
- Print the book
- Publish the PDF & printed version through Amazon.com and other possible sources
- Market

The backlog list is also not written in stone as it can be changed or pivoted over the progression of the project as needed.

Execution
Desire to Destination – D2D Marathon:

Many times when we start on something, the energy is high, but it slowly goes down after a few days or weeks. Keeping the energy high and doing what you want is the biggest challenge to overcome.

When you think about the final goal, it always looks like you are standing at the foot of Mt. Everest and wondering about how to reach the top.

Any huge goal cannot be achieved in a day or week, so we need to understand and accept it is going to take time and consistent effort to achieve it.

The biggest thought we need to keep at the top of our brain is to deliver value more often and more quickly. Sometimes it may not be perfect but over the course of execution it can be perfected.

Visualize the goal of reaching the summit as thousands of small steps. This can make us put our arms around the big vision.

In order to achieve the goal, I followed D2D Marathon.

The core concept of D2D Marathon is to think about determining a group of items to achieve in a week, then work on the items, and at the end of the week reflect on what went well, what didn't work, and what new things to adopt to improve in the upcoming week.

<u>**MVP: 1 – Release Plan 1**</u> – Release in 6 weeks – complete at least 6 chapters – minimum 3 chapters in principles and 3 chapters in patterns.

> ***A goal without a date is just a dream.***
> -Milton H. Erickson

Attaching a significance on the deadline, such as New Year, a birthday, wedding day, end of summer, before a vacation, etc., will also motivate you to work towards achieving the goal on time.

I started my book writing during the second week of April 2018 and I wanted to release my first MVP by the end of May 2018.

When I got a rush of thoughts, to prevent myself from forgetting them, I started writing in a notebook to try and capture them. I was able to incorporate these thoughts later on, when writing the chapters in my book.

I had limited time slots for myself, so I had to use time in the early mornings, late evenings and weekends to accomplish my goal. Every day, when I was able to contribute towards my weekly goal, I made sure to log in my Time Machine .

To write this book, I had to make a choice whether to use Microsoft Word, Google Docs or WordPress. Being acquainted with WordPress before (for a website I created for one of my friends), it was my default pick.

If you are not familiar with WordPress, it is the most widely used publishing/blogging platform and enables a lot of websites to start up quickly and it is available for free. One can easily get familiar with a publishing platform like WordPress by spending some time watching YouTube videos. There are also lots of books available to do more advanced things with WordPress.

I installed the WordPress tools on my PC and set up a website for writing the book, but there are also lots of online hosts available that don't need to be downloaded.

I did the entire first MVP in the local version, and when I was ready to publish it, I switched from my local PC version to the online version so that it was more maintainable and easy to share and review on the phone. This enabled me to get quick feedback from my reviewers.

For publishing the online version of this book, I used www.justhost.com because, in my opinion, they are comparatively cheaper and provided more features than other web hosts.

Since I already had the website name "www.DreamBigBuddy.com" registered, I started publishing the book chapters online for all to consume.

Risk mitigation: Make sure to save the work. Also, at the same time don't just depend on the local machine alone. The machine may crash and you might lose all your contents. I always took a backup using my email and also stored the files through an online data storage service called Dropbox.

Preplanning for the Sprint:

Determine what is the amount of time you can invest in the project and create a list of things you need to do. This doesn't have to be detailed, just take a few notes on what to accomplish. Ensure this is defined at the start of the week.

Release 1 – Tiny Execution – Sprint 1: Apr 30th – May 6th

I started with the introduction, which consisted of what this book is all about and why I am writing it. I already organized the book into 3 sections. Utilizing the notes from my notebook, I wrote my first chapter, "Life is a Gift" on May 1st, 2018 and I was very happy with the things I wrote. I felt motivated by completing the first chapter and I started collecting notes for the topics: "Time", "Money", and "Skill".

On May 4th, I finished writing the topic "Skill", and on May 6th, I was able to spend a good amount of time to finish the topic "Time".

I ended my first week sprint with a great sense of accomplishment and I was supercharged to write more chapters in the upcoming week sprint.

Reflection:

Every day when I looked at my Time Machine on how much time I invested, it gave me either a sub-conscious push to achieve more or a sense of satisfaction that I am doing great. So, I decided to practice my Time Machine consistently.

The early mornings on the weekends were the most effective times to work on this book, since I didn't have to think about office work. I told myself to utilize the early mornings on the weekends to the fullest.

Learning on a daily basis is also important to keep my creative thoughts flowing. I regularly made the practice of watching TED Talks and other informational videos during my evening workout time, while using the treadmill.

Preplan for the upcoming sprint: Finish more chapters

Release 1 – Tiny execution – Sprint 2: May 7th – May 13th

I started with a goal to write a few more chapters. During the weekdays, I didn't get much time to work on any chapters. My Time Machine was revealing that I was not putting time towards writing. So, I spent my weekend morning to write the chapters "Abundance" and "Adaptability".

Reflection:

Without Time Machine, I would have completely lost focus. I should continue to do Time Machine to ensure I am spending the needed time for the activities I want to achieve.

Preplan for the upcoming sprint: Finish a few chapters in Section 2: Patterns and Practices.

Release 1 – Tiny execution – Sprint 3: May 14th – May 20th

At the start of the week, I performed some editing on the already written chapters. Then, during that weekend, I was able to spend a good amount of time to work on my favorite chapter, "Time Machine".

Also, I finished the chapters on "Egg Hunt" and "Gauge and Grow" during that weekend.

I got an idea spark that before publishing my first MVP, I should have a cover design, because a picture can speak more than a thousand words.

I spent time and created the first cover design for the book. The design resembled a man with wings, which symbolized that when an individual realizes his/her own hidden potential, they can achieve great heights.

Reflection:

Continue Time Machine, since this pattern is working for me.

Preplan for the upcoming sprint: Prepare to publish the first MVP to a small circle of friends and family to get early feedback.

Release 1 – Tiny execution – Sprint 4: May 21st – May 27th

Worked on the chapters "Quotes", "Yogic Practices", "Dream Projector" and "Confront". Now, I had enough chapters in the book to convey my intent.

At that moment, all the content was in my local PC. To publish the content to my close group, as discussed before, I used JustHost.com. I took a backup of the local website from the PC and pushed the content to the JustHost online WordPress website.

Hereafter, I can now stop editing work in the local PC WordPress version, but rather, directly edit the online version. However, I still continued to take backups, so that I can avoid losing all of the data.

MVP Release:

MVP 1: Release Announcement & Feedback: May 26th & 27th

Utilizing the weekend, on May 26th, 2018, I announced that the first MVP of the book available on the website to a select group of friends and family who I could trust and get feedback from to help me in my journey.

If I publish it through Facebook or Twitter, it will be out to the whole world, but I wanted to share only to a small group. So, I utilized WhatsApp to send notifications to the select individuals.

I got a positive response from my trusted group on my efforts and some even gave me great feedback on the content, language usage and mistakes that I had to fix.

In the announcement, I had two things mentioned. I first talked about the coding club which I was doing and the second was the book. Since both were sent at the same time, the importance of the latter was not given much attention by many and they simply missed the link to the book. It was a great learning experience for me, that anytime I send out announcements I should convey what is the most important first.

All the feedback I got indicated that I was in the right direction and that I needed to continue the course towards completion.

Celebration: On May 27th, 2018, I celebrated the completion of MVP 1 by going out with family and I had a big sense of achievement.

The Making of: The Modern You – Uncover P3 – Part 2

Release 2 & 3 – Plan & Execution

Updated Backlog List to Complete the Book:

- Review the feedback from the initial reviewer circle and update the appropriate book
- Finish the remaining chapters
- Get feedback from the target audience
- Find the editors to handle the text editing for the whole book
- Engage a graphics designer to do the front and back covers
- Print the book
- Marketing

Quarterly Release Plan:

Every release plan should not exceed a maximum time period of 1 quarter (3 months). Some follow monthly release plans. It is based on your choice. My recommendation would be to keep a quarterly cycle.

Inside each quarterly cycle, execute the work in small batches called "Tiny Executions". I adopted weekly executions for this book project. Optionally, you can do bi-weekly periods. The important thing to keep in mind is at the end of each Tiny Execution, whatever was worked on, needs to reach a completion stage. Always strive to work towards completion.

Having a release cycle for more than one quarter diminishes the focus on the release goal date as it gives the impression that you have a very long time to handle things.

Pictorial Representation

<u>**A Journey - The Making of the Book**</u>
<u>**Release 2**</u>

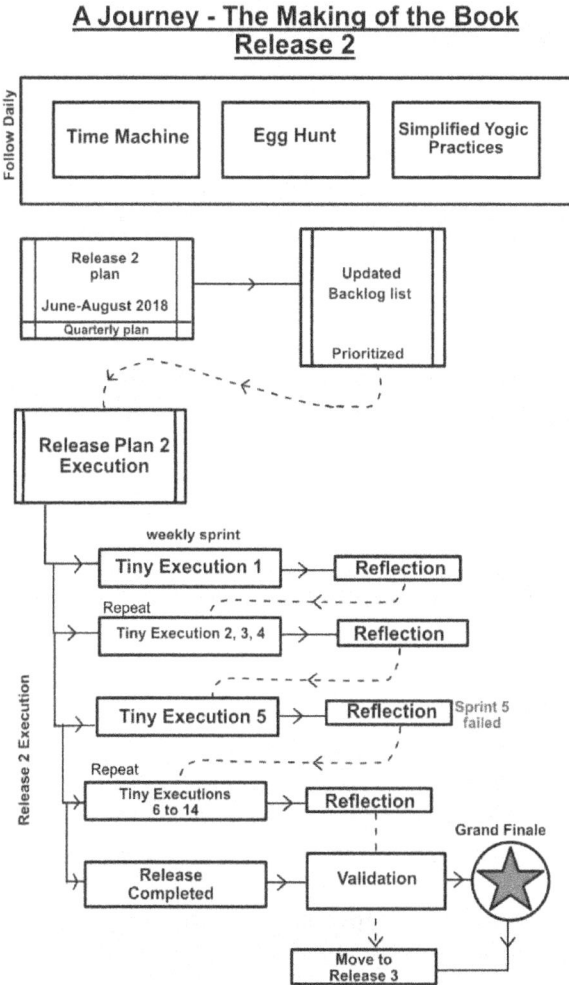

Refer Section 2, to understand the patterns such as Time Machine, Egg Hunt, Dream Projector, D2D Marathon, and Grand Finale.

Release Plan 2: June – August 2018

Top priority items picked from the backlog list for the Release Plan 2:

- Utilize the feedback from the initial reviewer circle and update the book accordingly
- Finish the remaining chapters
- Get feedback from the target audience
- Find the editors to handle the text edit for the whole book

Also, whatever worked well on Release Plan 1, follow them.

Release Plan 2 – Tiny Execution 1: May 28th – June 3rd

Wrote chapters "Moral Loan" and "Disruption" (now "New Normals").

Release Plan 2 – Tiny Execution 2: June 4th – June 10th

Used Grammarly to review all the content written so far and corrected the grammar and word usage.

To keep the interest high from my early reviewers, I created the back cover page to nudge them to read more.

A picture can speak a thousand words. For the reader to quickly understand the scope of the book, I made a one-page infographics.

Release Plan 2 – Tiny Execution 3: *June 11th – June 17th*

Wrote chapters "Work", "Blame", "Border Wall", and "Carousel".

Release Plan 2 – Tiny Execution 4: *June 18th – June 24th*

Began the chapter "Thinker Muscles" and also spent a good amount of time editing the previously completed chapters.

Release Plan 2 – Tiny Execution 5: *June 25th – Jul 1st*

No time spent on writing the book this week because I had to handle some family-related issues, but by logging the information in Time Machine, I was able to quickly get back on track.

Reflection: Sprint failed

Release Plan 2 – Tiny Execution 6: *Jul 2nd – Jul 8th*

Worked on chapters "Entrepreneurship" and "Thinker Muscles".

Release Plan 2 – Tiny Execution 7: Jul 9th – Jul 15th

More edits on the previously edited topics.

Got an email from one of my friends' daughter, Aiswaryaa, that she liked the content but it needs to be edited. Also got similar feedback from another high schooler, Sengathir.

I asked them whether they can work with me to edit the book. They gladly agreed to become the official student editors for the book. Because they were on vacation they were not available to immediately start, but they were able to come starting mid-August. What great timing!

Now, I needed to plan on finishing all the chapters so I can fully engage in the editing process.

Release Plan 2 – Tiny Execution 8: Jul 16th – Jul 22nd

Wrote "Grand Finale" and edited "Entrepreneurship".

Release Plan 2 – Tiny Execution 9: Jul 23rd – Jul 29th

No work was done on the book – because of a work emergency undertaken in the office, which had to be delivered within a week, so I had to put extra hours.

Reflection: Sprint failed

Release Plan 2 – Tiny Execution 10: Jul 30th – Aug 5th

Spent more time on learning (using Egg Hunt), but no time put into working on the book

Reflection: Sprint failed

Release Plan 2 – Tiny Execution 11: Aug 6th – Aug 12th

Went on a family vacation, which was previously planned, so no time put into writing.

Being conscious of these non-commitments of time and continuously logging that into the Time Machine, it was creating a guilty feeling of not putting any work towards my dream.

Reflection: Sprint failed

Release Plan 2 – Tiny Execution 12: Aug 13th – Aug 19th

Started back where I left off and updated chapters "Time Machine" and "Entrepreneurship".

Release Plan 2 – Tiny Execution 13: Aug 20th – Aug 26th

Spent a good amount of time editing the contents of the completed topics while working with Aiswaryaa and Sengathir.

Edited topics "Introduction", "Target Audience", "Life is a Gift", "Time", "Skill", "Energy", "Abundance", and "Adaptability".

It was a good opportunity for me to learn from the target audience, such as how they perceive things, fix grammar errors, and sometimes change the way it is framed.

I even changed the name of one of the topics from "Disruptions" to "New Normals" after a good discussion with Sengathir and Aiswaryaa.

Also it was a mutual benefit for them since they were hearing first-hand about the content directly from me and discussed the topics in detail to get more clarity on why I wrote and what I wrote.

Reflection: Great progress

Release Plan 2 – Tiny Execution 14: _Aug 27th – Sep 2nd_

Edited some more chapters and we were able to successfully finish all the chapters in Section 1.

At this point in time I had only two chapters left to write in Section 2.

Release 2 – Ending

I am close to completing the goal of finishing the writing, but there are still two chapters yet to be completed.

On the editing front, half the book is edited. However, I didn't expect that this would take a long time.

Doing Time Machine was a big help in keeping me focused. Following the D2D Marathon consistently helped me to ensure to check on the progress towards the growth on a weekly timebox.

Updated Backlog List to Complete the Book:

- Finish the remaining two chapters in Section 2
- Finish the edits for Section 2 and Closing
- Engage a graphics designer to do the front and back covers
- Print the book and Market

Release Plan 3: September – November 2018

Pictorial Representation

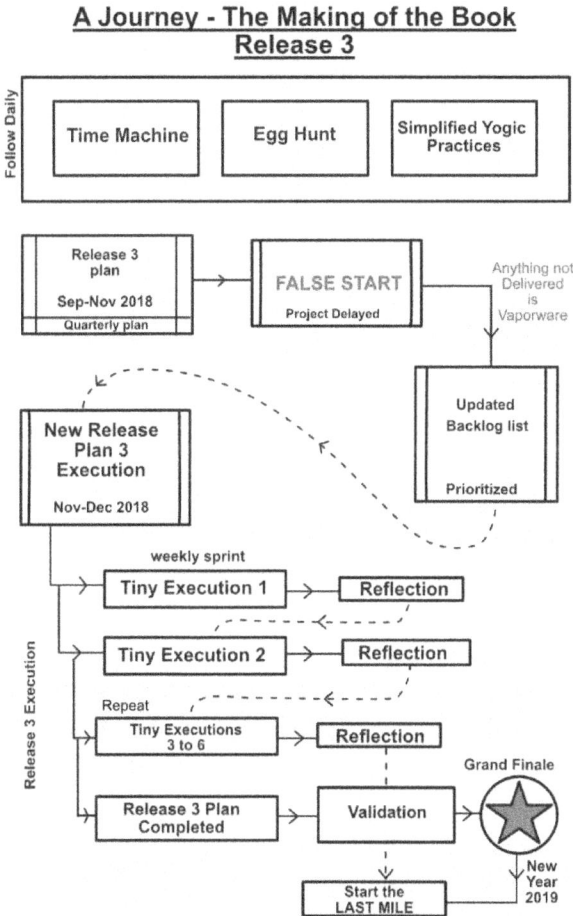

A Journey - The Making of the Book Release 3

Refer Section 2, to understand the patterns such as Time Machine, Egg Hunt, Dream Projector, D2D Marathon, and Grand Finale.

Normally September and October are the months I get super busy with office work since we work towards a user conference where we present what we have done since the last conference.

Also, I went through an unexpected medical condition which put me into a situation where I was not able to continue writing the book.

Fear freezes action.

In the computer industry, customers call the undelivered product as Vaporware or Smokeware. If the planned work is not completed and not delivered in a way that can be used by your intended audience, it just costs you more money to have it held as inventory.

Anything not delivered to customers is Vaporware. It's just inventory and is worth zero plus it costs money to keep it.

Have you ever realized that you are always given more deals at the end of the season sale? Sometimes the sale can be 50%, 70%, or even 90% as the days go on. Why are there sales? What are the companies trying to achieve?

By keeping it in the store, it is inventory. It is taking physical space to store and has to be managed, and at the same time, it may get old and lose its significance. It all costs money. It is economical to sell it cheaper than to keep it.

Inventory costs money and resources. Inventory is expensive.

At this time, this book was just inventory because it was continuing to cost me money to host it but was not yet ready for publication.

Having written this book so far and reading the chapters over again gave me the boost to keep working on the book starting from mid-November with the same energy I had before.

Release Plan 3: Extended till December 31st 2018 to finish the planned.

__Release Plan 3 – Tiny Execution 1:__ Nov 19th – Nov 25th

Worked on editing "Yogic Practices". While I kept working on the book, I also shared this to more of my friends who could provide feedback. I was talking to my cousin and asked him if his son, Pranav, a high schooler, could also assist in doing the edits.

Pranav reviewed the book and sent me the edits for Section 1.

Reflection: Good progress after a long break.

- Fear freezes action – inaction doesn't help, we have to move on.
- Inaction is only in the mind, so get out of the downward spiral quickly.

- Time Machine is a need – whether you do action or don't take action, this gives a lot of valuable insight and it pushes you forward.

Release Plan 3 – Tiny Execution 2: **Nov 26th – Dec 2nd**

After reviewing the edits from Pranav, I updated them in the book.

Worked on creating the first PDF which can provide me with some insight on how the printed book will be like.

I needed some way to print the book, so after doing some research, I found a website, blurb.com. This website does the logistics of taking the software source copy (PDF/blurb file) of the book and doing the printing, shipping and also selling automatically in Amazon. By utilizing this service, I can self-publish my book.

I learned that every book needs an ISBN number and a separate barcode for printing and to sell the online PDF version through Amazon or other book stores.

Even though both are important, I don't have to rush in spending the money until I really need to. After all, I know I am only halfway done with the book.

Reflection: Good progress and lot of new learnings

Release Plan 3 – Tiny Execution 3: **Dec 3rd – Dec 9th**

Started writing on the topic, "The Making of the Book".

For the Headstream club activities, to get more support, I wanted to come up with a way to self-motivate all the students. At first, I thought of printing T-shirts, but finally decided to create "Tribal Bands".

Aspirant Tribal Bands

There are several online sites to print the bands in different styles and sizes. I was able to get it ordered within 2 hours from getting the initial idea.

Technology kept proving to me again and again how it is an enabler.

Reflection: Good progress

Release Plan 3 – Tiny Execution 4: *Dec 10th – Dec 16th*

Expanded the topic "Quotes" with Ekalavya. Felt very good on the way the topic came out.

Reflection: Good progress

Release Plan 3 – Tiny Execution 5: *Dec 17th – Dec 23rd*

Updated the topic "Everything Starts with a Dream".

Finished editing the topic "Egg Hunt" along with Aiswaryaa and Sengathir.

Created a concept sketch for the book, so that I can give it to the graphic designer and create a professional front and back cover for the book.

Reflection: Good progress

Release Plan 3 – Tiny Execution 6: *Dec 24h – Dec 31st*

As this whole week was a vacation, I decided I should utilize my time to the fullest by completing the edits of Section 2, and also finished writing the chapter on "The Making of the Book".

Expanded the topic "Yogic Practices" by adding a sub-topic called "Vibrant Colors of Life".

Worked with Sengathir and Aiswaryaa to completely finish the edits in Section 2.

The chapter on the making of the book seems to require more content, so I decided to move that to its own section.

Reflection: Editing the whole of Section 2 is completed. Overall great progress.

Release 3 – Ending

The goal of Section 2 is completed, with the exception of not being able to finish writing the chapter
"Application of the Patterns and Practices: A Journey...". But now that I moved that chapter to its own section, I have decided to take it up in the next release cycle.

Celebration: Whole of Section 1 and Section 2 is fully done, which is 31 chapters, including the book's introduction. I had a great sense of accomplishment.

Even though the book is not fully done, the small progress done regularly over a long period of time has brought me close to reaching the summit.

Being that it is a new year, I decided to give an Amazon gift card to my student editors Aiswaryaa, Sengathir and Pranav to wish them big in their lives and as a way to tell them "Thank you".

Release Cycle reviews gives you an opportunity to understand your position and provides an opportunity to steer for forward motion. By celebrating your achievement, it gives the necessary boost for you to achieve the next mile.

The making of: The Modern You – Uncover P3 – Part 3 – The Last Mile

Release Plan 4: January 2019 – March 2019

Updated Backlog List to Complete the Book:

- Finish the last section – the making of the book
- Create a full PDF version and do complete book review/edits.
- Engage a graphic designer to do the front and back covers
- Push the Amazon Kindle version for sale
- Print the book and make it available through Amazon.com
- Market

The writing of this section 3 is very interesting because of the fact that I need to write about how I wrote the book. Indeed, this chapter "The Last Mile", is intriguing because it is about writing on how I wrote the making of the book (Section3).

In computer programming it is called
Recursion. *It's challenging and fun to identify and cod e recursions.*

Section 3 is a recollection of how I had been working on the book for the past nine months, and it was easy for me to do, since I have been following the Time Machine and writing key pointers regularly.

Pictorial Representation

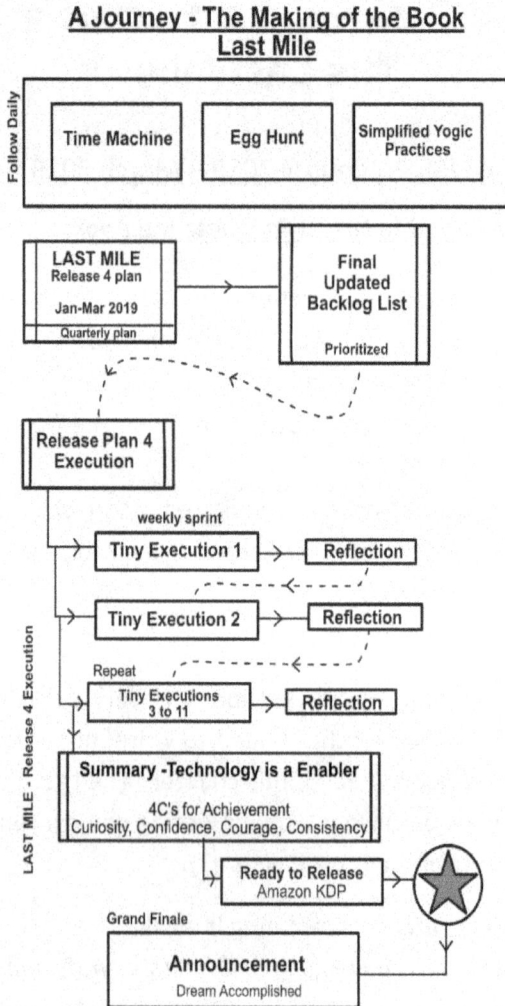

A Journey - The Making of the Book Last Mile

Follow Daily

Time Machine	Egg Hunt	Simplified Yogic Practices

LAST MILE
Release 4 plan

Jan-Mar 2019

Quarterly plan

→

Final Updated Backlog List

Prioritized

Release Plan 4 Execution

LAST MILE - Release 4 Execution

weekly sprint

Tiny Execution 1 → Reflection

Tiny Execution 2 → Reflection

Repeat

Tiny Executions 3 to 11 → Reflection

Summary -Technology is a Enabler

4C's for Achievement
Curiosity, Confidence, Courage, Consistency

Ready to Release
Amazon KDP

Grand Finale

Announcement
Dream Accomplished

Refer Section 2, to understand the patterns such as Time Machine, Egg Hunt, Dream Projector, D2D Marathon, and Grand Finale.

Release Plan 4 – Tiny Execution 1: Jan 1st – Jan 6th

Finished the making of the book – chapter 1, "Inception, Planning and Execution – MVP release" and worked with Sengathir to edit that chapter.

Added competency ladder to the chapter "Skill".

An updated chapters using review comments from Pranav on the topic "Preface", "Target Audience" and "Author".

Release Plan 4 – Tiny Execution 2: Jan 7th – Jan 13th

Did some edits on the topic "Life is a Gift".

Started writing on the Release 3. During this time was my biggest delay in my execution. Writing about it gave me more focus and strengthened on how to avoid negative spirals.

Release Plan 4 – Tiny Execution 3: Jan 14th – Jan 20th

Finished writing on Release 3.

On weekends, I worked with Aiswaryaa, Sengathir and Tharunika to edit the complete chapter on Release 2 & 3.

Release Plan 4 – Tiny Execution 4: Jan 21st – Jan 27th

Created the backlog list for Release 4 and finished topic Tiny Execution 1.

Release Plan 4 – Tiny Execution 5: *Jan 28th – Feb 3rd*

Updated topic on Time and D2D Marathon.

Finished topics Tiny Executions 2, 3, and 4.

Felt I should write a topic on, "Success and Failure". Added a new topic under Principles (Section 1).

Release Plan 4 – Tiny Execution 6: *Feb 4th – Feb 10th*

No time spent on working on the book.

Sprint failed.

Release Plan 4 – Tiny Execution 7: *Feb 11th – Feb 17th*

Updated "Entrepreneurship" with a paragraph on Quality.

Completed the topic "Success and Failure".

Created a full PDF version of the book to see the layout and how much it will cost for the printing.

Initiated the graphic design for the cover page design using Fiverr.com

Release Plan 4 – Tiny Execution 8: *Feb 18th – Feb 24th*

Reviewed the designs from the graphics designer and provided feedback for correction. Graphics designers always have a magical touch to make the things look great. At this moment, I am very happy with the direction the cover page design is heading towards.

Continue to update "The Last Mile" with notes related to how technology enabled me in writing this book.

Consolidated the information from student editors and updated the "Students Editor" chapter.

Release Plan 4 – Tiny Execution 9: Feb 25th – Mar 3rd

Initiated professional editing using fiverr.com

Release Plan 4 – Tiny Execution 10: Mar 4th – Mar 10th

Consolidated the edits and preparing the final manuscript for the formatting to publish.

Continue to review the back cover design from the graphic designer and provided feedback for modifications.

Release Plan 4 – Tiny Execution 11: Mar 11th – Mar 17th

Finalized the cover design.

Finished the formatting for to get ready for printing and online release through Amazon KDP.

Release Plan 4 – Announcement – Grand Finale

Planned to release the book on Tamil Newyears' Day celebration function hosted by South Jersey Tamil Association (SJTA).

SJTA is a non-profit focused on teaching tamil language to the kids in south jersey, USA

Technology is an Enabler:

From the start to the end of this book technology was utilized to make the journey easier and faster.

- **YouTube** was utilized as a primary source to do "Egg Hunt".
- **WordPress** is utilized to make the website (very little effort is required to create pages and blogs – no software knowledge required to get started and you can do lot more things with that, like running your own ecommerce website etc.).
- Hosted the website using **JustHost.com**.
- **Name.com** was utilized to purchase the name for the website.
- **SnagIt** was used to create infographics – it's a very simple tool to create quick illustrations.
- **Affinity Designer** was used to create the final print ready infographics and the flowcharts.
- **WhatsApp** for spreading the message to closed groups and getting quick feedback
- **GMail** for sending emails between my student editors and taking file backups

- **Dropbox** for taking website & file backups
- **Grammarly** was used to correct some of the writing. *[My student editors came handy and did the heavy lifting to fix the issues]*.
- **Microsoft Word** was used for doing editing and track changes.
- **FreeMind** was used to create the Mind Map of the book.
- **Fiverr.com** was utilized to hire freelancers for cover page design, professional editing and formatting. Its worth outsourcing for to fill your gaps and to achieve professional output in your works.
- **Amazon Kindle Direct Publishing (KDP)** is utilized for publishing the book online version through amazon kindle and they also have paperback printing option at a very affordable cost.

Utilizing these technologies makes the job to be handled immediately. Also it is very affordable, The cost I incurred to make this book was less than 500$.

5 to 10 years ago, this would have cost ten times the cost I incurred today.

We all have these tools in hand and they are going to get better. So there is no need to wait. You simply need to start and try to use more of the technology to help your journey to achieve your destination quickly.

Summary

Over the period of last 10 months, I was doing activities in small steps and now it is in front of me as a huge endeavor, I was able to achieve this with ease.

Making of this book became a reality by keeping the 4C of Walt Disney (Curiosity, Confidence, Courage, and Constancy) at heart all the time and executed during the whole time.

Following the patterns helped me, not to deviate from the course and able to achieve my end goal.

I can more than 100% sure you can achieve by adopting the patterns and executing them until the goal is reached.

SECTION 4 – CLOSING

Confront

Confront yourself – What do I really want?

Am I living my dream life?

- Am I working towards my dream?
- Am I living for somebody else's dream, or do I not know?

You can wait for a later time to explore and experiment, only if you strongly believe in the next generation. Personally, I am not sure it even exists.

What we have currently is real. For how long is unsure.

Winners made the stories of history. Even the losers are part of history.
But spectators and gossipers don't have a single line.

What is the biggest project you can think of than "living your life the way you want"? You have the choice to design your life the way you want, or you can live as it unfolds.

The choice is powerful. It has two sides: choosing or not choosing. Both are choices we always have.

Waiting for luck to make magic is the choice of NOT trying to take ownership of your outcome, and instead, live a lazy life. It does work out for some, but the probability is very low.

Have you ever tried to answer the question:

What is the value of your life?

Take a look at history and see what was the value of the lives of the great achievers in their early lives, before their achievement and after.

> *"Value has a value only if its value is valued."*
> — Bryan Dyson

Even though money is important, whatever you do should be fulfilled from within.

In life, work, family, health, friends, and spirit are all equally important, and we shouldn't trade one for the other.

Insanity: *Doing the same thing again and again, expecting different results.*

Learning with no action is a waste. There is no shortcut to success. It requires sacrifice, work, and focus.

Death is inevitable; every day is a bonus.

Every event that happens in your life, however small or insignificant, holds the potential to change your future forever.

Nobody is restricted by anything.

How you want to live is ultimately your choice.

"In the end, we regret only the chances we didn't take."
– Lewis Carroll

Life is a gift!

Show the world what you can do.

"Arise! Awake! and stop not until the goal is reached."
– Swami Vivekananda

Everything Starts
With a Dream

A dream is not just the thing you see in your sleep, but it is also the thing that doesn't let you sleep.

Everything starts with a dream. Don't wait to sleep to start dreaming.

There is always another chance for everything in life. But the fact is, there is no chance of another life...

Do it while you can. There is no perfect time to start. Don't wait, start now, create your perfect time.

"It starts with a dream.

Add faith, and it becomes a belief.

Add Action, and it becomes a part of life.

Add perseverance, and it becomes a goal in sight.

Add patience and time, and it ends with a dream come true."

- Doe Zantamata

"You have to dream
before your dreams can come true."
– Dr. A. P. J. Abdul Kalam

Appendix

*Application of the principles, patterns, and
practices in Headstream project
(Dream to Destination
Work-in-progress)*

Headstream - Dream Big Buddy Coding Club

I Believe:

Any skill learned early on can take you to miraculous destinations which you never dreamed of !!

Purpose:

- Gamify learning to make the learning fun and rewarding.

- Make technology education accessible and affordable to all in the world.

Our philosophy to succeed:

- Through FUN understand FUNDAMENTALS
- Create CURIOSITY to build CHARACTER
- Nurture INTEREST to make INNOVATION

By emphasizing the above in our practices, we will empower the next generation to realize their fullest potential and to create their dream life.

How "Headstream" started:

Bill Gates started programming when he was 10 and made his first game when he was 13. He made computers accessible to the masses through his company Microsoft.

Eben Upton at the age of 15 built his first robot. He built the world's smallest and cheapest computer called "Raspberry Pi" at the age of 35.

Inspired by the power of computers and the life stories of Bill Gates & Eben Upton, I realized that still a huge population doesn't have this knowledge or the awareness of the latest trends. So, I felt the need to do something to fill this gap. I should do something to bring the coding skill to kids at a very early age so that they have a shot to do something like Bill Gates and Eben Upton to the world.

Dream:

This idea sparked in the fall of 2015 and as always I started writing down the thoughts of what I wanted to do in a notebook. In this book "The modern You", I call this method "Dream Projector".

In 2016, during my free time, I first started working with my daughter who was in 1st grade at that time to introduce programming and she started liking it. we started with Scratch Programming, which is an open source(free) tool to introduce programming to beginners.

Dream to Desire:

During this process, I learned many things and thought I could teach other kids also and told my known circle of friends. They were very happy to send their kids for this program, and I started creating workbooks for the classes by doing small steps for a few hours every week. We started off with 1 class per week and I send the material through email so the kids can take a printout and bring it to the classes.

At the end of 2016, one of the parents gave me a letter, which was written by his son in school because his teacher asked his class to write one for "Thanksgiving". I never expected that letter and it made me realize I am on to something <u>bigger than myself</u>, and that I should take this to a much bigger level and make it accessible for all.

Desire to Destination:
Dream Big Coding Club – "Headstream":

Headstream: a stream that is the source of a river

We are regularly conducting classes every Monday evening 7:30 PM to 8:30PM for 2 years now.

Having created a syllabus for 2 years to teach programming and the vision for the future, it is time to take this to the next level.

To make this accessible to all deserving kids, we need to replicate this into several clubs and do this all over the world. The first club we started here, "Headstream", will provide the guidance and support to all future clubs so that each club can make a difference in their local area.

Coaching materials we have created so far:

- Level 1 – Intro to Scratch Programming
- Level 2 – Advanced Scratch programming
- Level 3 – Python programming
- Level 4 – Programming the Raspberry Pi & fun with electronics
- Level 5 - Advanced Programming concepts
- Level 6 - Power of the Internet - Start your first internet blog, website, business

- Books
  - The Modern You – Uncover P3 (Principles, Patterns, & Practices to achieve your dreams)

What we are doing through "Headstream - Dream Big Buddy Coding Club":

- Conduct coding classes
- Provide course completion awards
- Create training videos
- Build the innovator generation
- Conduct annual events and fun

You are welcome to join our TRIBE **– "Dream Big Buddy Coding Club":**

- Send an email to **tribe@dreambigbuddy.com** to show your support
- https://www.dreambigbuddy.com/dbbheadstream/

Student Editors

Aiswaryaa Prabaharan

My name is Aiswaryaa Prabhakaran, I am a sophomore at Lenape High School, New Jersey. My hobbies include listening to music, reading, and drawing. I spend lots of time wondering about anything and everything, and I am very creative. At school, I am part of the robotics team, involved in two science clubs, and am a member of student council. I am keeping my options open for the future by taking a variety of challenging classes at school.

Sengathir Rajagopal

I am Sengathir Rajagopal, I am a sophomore at Lanepe High School. I am involved in several activities in and out of my school. I participate in chess club, robotics, as well as the Science League and ChemClub offered at my school. Additionally, I use my time out of school to volunteer and learn music. During my free time, I like to draw and listen to music. My ambition for my future is to go into the medical field.

Pranav Raj

My name is Pranav Raj and I'm a sophomore in McKinney, Texas. I run on track, play basketball, and participate in several extracurricular clubs. One day I'd like to create my own company and revolutionize the world. Until that day, I'm doing everything I can to reach that goal!

Tharunika Govindasamy

Hi! My name is Tharunika Govindasamy. I am a freshman at Cherry Hill East. I play soccer for Cherry Hill FC and try to dabble in other sports such as basketball and volleyball. Singing is an enjoyment of mine as I take Carnatic vocal lessons outside of school and sing with my peers in school. English has always been a strong point of mine while Math...let's just say is not it. My passion for writing has been with me since a very young age. I even started a blog when I was in second grade, thinking that I was famous and "made it"! Down the line in a couple of years, I hope to achieve my goal of becoming a criminal lawyer and to also play college soccer. Hopefully, I will have the chance to strengthen my writing skills by investing more time into that field. I am very thankful for having the chance to edit this extraordinary novel with the creative author and my fellow editors.

Acknowledgements

First of all, big thanks to Mr. Bala V Satyanarayanan a well-established thought leader, currently serving as CHRO at Greif Inc, for gladly accepting to write the foreword for this book. He's also a recipient of the following awards

- 2018 HR Hero - Elevating the Strategic Role Of HR
- Outstanding 50 Asian Americans in Business

Special thanks to my student editors who helped me in reviewing and editing the first cut and I greatly appreciate you all for spending time with me during the summer vacation and also during the weekends for the last eight months working on the book. I had great fun discussing the topics with you all and explaining the concepts.

Thanks to all my friends and family members who were very supportive in this journey.

Special thanks to Uthaman, Praba Ponnusamy, Kamal, Jai Vani, Sundar, Arun Prasad, KP Ganesh, JK Bala, Prasy, Dr. Rao, Dhilip Kumar, Mihir Parekh, Ramesh, Ravi Gade, Raghu, Kevin, Alexys, Dr. Anirudhan, Dr. Sri Lakshmi, Bala. K, Mr. Ramesh Viswanathan and Mr. Muthumani for going way beyond reviewing the text and providing me with their opinions and valuable insights which helped in shaping this book.

Finally, I'd like to express my gratitude to my wife Bhuvanya for putting her design skills at work in doing the process flow diagrams for Section 4 and book infographics using Affinity Designer and importantly being extremely supportive throughout this journey to accomplish this huge dream of mine.

About the Author

I am Naren Asokaraju,

A Dreamer, Creative Driver, Futurist, Software Craftsman, Teacher, Aspiring Author, and Fun Lover.

As a VP of Engineering, driving innovations and leading a technology team of 180 members developing public safety software at ProPhoenix Corporation, serving 400+ police departments in the USA.

Lucky husband and father of 2 little girls.

Graced with a big circle of very supportive friends, cousins, and family group.

My Moral Loan - Payback:

10% of the proceeds from this book will be donated to selected Charites working on providing education to the underprivileged kids all over the world (such as Tamilnadu Foundation (TNF)).

By purchasing this book for yourself or as a gift to an aspirant, you are automatically joining hands with me in this needed movement of giving back to the society called "Moral Loan Web".

What is Moral Loan?

Please refer the chapter "Moral Loan", under Section 1: Principles

---

www.ingramcontent.com/pod-product-compliance
Lightning Source LLC
Chambersburg PA
CBHW021124020426
42331CB00005B/624